TITUS 2 WOMAN

WOMAN 2 WOMAN

A Teacher's Study Guide

R.J. Miller

WestBow Press books may be ordered through booksellers or by contacting:

WestBow Press
A Division of Thomas Nelson & Zondervan
1663 Liberty Drive
Bloomington, IN 47403
www.westbowpress.com
844-714-3454

ISBN: 978-1-6642-9500-1 (sc)
ISBN: 978-1-6642-9501-8 (e)

Library of Congress Control Number: 2023904695

Print information available on the last page.

WestBow Press rev. date: 04/13/2023

Contents

ACKNOWLEDGEMENTS

This study was first formed in about 1993. When preacher, pastor, and teacher, Dr. Lon Stewart, was teaching the book of Titus to the church. During one particular teaching he *challenged* the women of the church to teach the things which are listed in Titus 2:3–5. He was serious about this challenge. R.J. Miller along with other women from the church heard this call and took it to heart, they saw the wisdom in its teaching. Even though many of them were still baby Christians themselves they did what they could. Not long after that he asked the women to make a syllabus for the teaching. This study guide is the result of that challenge, the syllabus, and from teaching this over the years.

Besides Brother Lon, women who were aged or very aged, offered counsel and their wisdom for this study and they should be acknowledged. Thank you and love to; Lorrie, Alice, Cathy, Bess, Bobbeye, Marion, Jean, Winona, Gwen, Dianne, Lisa, Claudia and so many others who through their kindheartedness bore through these lessons. They helped to continue this earnest quest for the knowledge of God's will in this teaching. Praise the Lord for them.

R.J. has felt a very strong urging from the Lord to make this work available to all Christian women. May each of you also be challenged by the wisdom of its teaching. And may it spark a desire in you to please Jesus, our Lord and Savior to teach, to learn, and to love.

Titus 2 Woman 2 Woman

"The aged women likewise, that they be in behavior as becometh holiness, not false accusers, not given to much wine, teachers of good things; that they teach the young women to be sober, to love their husbands, to love their children, to be discreet, chaste, keepers at home, good, obedient to their own husbands, that the word of God be not blasphemed." Titus 2:3–5

This study is not about any one person. It is about GOD and His plan for His women. Remember God's forgiveness, truth, and grace is in His Son!

INTRODUCTION

What is this study about?

This study is meant to be used as a guide for teaching and learning God's plan for Christian women as directed to us in the Book of Titus, Chapter 2:3–5. It is meant to equip the saints, especially aged women for this teaching. Overall, it can help to sanctify the woman believer and set her apart from women of the world. If we are willing and prepared vessels God's plan can be fulfilled in us. The study outlines each of the godly qualities and instructions to us on an individual word study basis. It is our hope and prayer that through this study God will put each of these qualities to work in our lives for His sake, for His women and the church, "*That He might sanctify and cleanse it with the washing of water by the word.*" Ephesians 5:26. Then with the power of the Holy Spirit instilling God's love and grace through us, it should initiate ripples of love and understanding into the body of Christ and yield the peaceable fruit of His Spirit.

Who should do this study?

Aged women should do this study, it is a tool meant to help 'aged' women gain confidence in this area of ministry. And show aged women how He will equip and prepare us when we encounter most questions that could come up in its teaching. And young women should do this study to be encouraged in their walk with the Lord. All Christian women will appreciate the help and friendship of fellow Christian women as they converse about the topics which will be addressed. This study is for saved women, who desire to know what God wants to teach us. And with the guidance of the Holy Spirit, it will have meaning for us.

Saved from what? From eternal separation from God. Knowing that there is a God, who created all things and sent His Son to save us from our sins. It is our sin that separates us from God. Do we really know Jesus as our Savior? Has our mind changed to agree with what God said sin is and turn from it? Sin is what each of us do that is against God and His nature. Have we asked Him for forgiveness of our sins? God wants us to believe in His plan of salvation, that by sending His Son, Jesus, to pay the price for our sins by His death, burial, and resurrection we can be saved. It is *only* through Jesus that God will accept us into His kingdom. If we have confessed this with our mouth and believe it in our heart, God will never leave us nor forsake us. Once saved we can look to Jesus for all our hopes and needs and know that we are a member of the family of God.

Those who have not accepted Christ, should know that it is the Lord's will for us to be saved. According to 2 Peter 3:9, "*The Lord is not slack concerning his promise, as some men count slackness; but is longsuffering to us-ward, not willing that any should perish, but that all should come to repentance.*" Prayers can be said anytime to God to ask for His salvation. Any saved Pastor, Christian woman or other Christian should be happy to pray and help lead us to the saving grace of our Lord Jesus Christ. If not, they should find someone to lead us in the acceptance of God's grace to us. "*And this is the confidence that we have in him, that, if we ask any thing according to his will, he heareth us.*" 1 John 5:14.

Why should we teach this study?

God has set standards for Christian women, His women. He has also given us the ability to achieve these standards by the power of His Holy Spirit and through the guidance of His Word. We should teach this study because it is outlined in Titus 2 and God is the rewarder of all who diligently seek Him. There are many churches that have women's ministries; Bible studies, Nursery work, serving meals, and teaching Sunday School. But this particular ministry is usually lacking in our churches. And women seem to slip through God's loving arms and sometimes even leave the church. One reason this happens is because they are not being fulfilled by the friendships of other Christian women and the true teaching about their role as a woman of God.

Once a woman becomes a believer, important doctrines need to be learned, such as Baptism and Communion and Discipleship which churches teach on a regular basis. Women's Bible study is also great for new believers. Through this study we learn the reasons for this lack of teaching and how to continue with our journey in Christ. It covers every facet of our being from His word and how each of these facets; body, mind and spirit are to be geared by Him for His glory. He helps us be prepared to face every role we have as women, in a godly fashion. Just as with all Bible Study, every time we read and study His word, we find new and deeper meaning.

His plan not only shows a better way of life for us, but also for our families and all Christian women. When these lessons are practiced by us, they will affect the world around us. They will distinctively show Gods glory in this world. These lessons also prepare us for that day in which we will meet our Savior, standing before Him at the seat where He will judge our Christian works. Before we begin to teach the Titus 2 Woman pray and ask the Holy Spirit to anoint our hearts with and guide us all in all understanding.

This study is not about any 'one' person and their faults or sins or even their holiness. It is about God's plan for His women. Keep in mind through this study that the Bible states we are not to think more highly of ourselves than we ought. We are not God, He is. And yet because we are forgiven and are members of the family of God, we should not think too lowly of ourselves either. This study is meant as a *tool* to share each lesson by initiating conversation between aged and young women, this conversation is of great price. To share our personal testimonies and tell how we have put our faith in Christ into practice and even how at times we have failed, but God was faithful.

The decision to write this study guide is because of a strong urging from the Lord and because Christian women have followed Gods will for their lives and led rich lives due to it. It has also been written because too many Christian women did not follow Christ and His teachings and now realize through salvation and the knowledge of God and His word, that they suffered many needless and hurtful things. They now want to share the truth of His excellent plan of grace and forgiveness.

Some women question whether they are to share this biblical information to people they do not know. If a person says they are a Christian, we should accept their word for it. We cannot judge people's heart. God will be the judge of that. We should do our job with our own right heart attitude for His kingdom. Hopefully the Lord will make known a person's intentions and they will recognize their need for salvation if they are not saved. All Christian women should know the truth of this study.

Women need encouragement about their decisions, in Christ. Women who have a *sincere desire* to know God's plan for their lives and want to know how to achieve it will appreciate this study. Trusting God to accomplish His will in us we women are given the opportunity to follow Jesus. We know it is our faith alone, in Jesus, that pleases God. See Hebrews 11:6. His plan is the same for all Christian women. We should understand this more as we learn from the following lessons and grow closer to the Lord and each other, in confidences and love. The footnote on the first page of each section is a reminder of God's forgiveness, grace, and for our encouragement.

If all *aged* women would teach at least one *young* woman and our own daughters, a significant impact would be made on the family of God. Without this important teaching we women, as the weaker vessels (see I Peter 3:7) might feel we stand alone and have no power over the world or ourselves. But together we can accomplish much for His glory. Why should any Christian women risk Satan sifting us like wheat (Luke 22:31), losing our savor as the salt of the earth (Matthew 5:13) or becoming as a jewel of gold, in a swine's snout (Proverbs 11:22) not having discretion before God and in our lives? Even if we have experienced those things and feel useless, we can ask forgiveness and now do as God asks us. "*I can do all things through Christ, which strengtheneth me*". Philippians 4:13. He wants His women to be strengthened together. We should ask ourselves if we are willing to be a vessel for His teaching other women? Are we willing to be taught?

When and How do we begin?

Once deciding on the importance of this ministry, speak to the pastor of your church for guidance. The pastor, deacons or other teachers should be able to direct newer Christian women to the study. Before beginning each lesson, pray that the Holy Spirit will guide and give us understanding. Pray also that anyone studying or leading these lessons, will have the courage and commitment to follow the guidelines and apply them to their own life. Each woman will need a copy of the Holy Bible. All scripture used was studied from the *Authorized King James Version*. The *Strong's Exhaustive Concordance, Vine's Dictionary, Webster's Dictionary, All the Women of the Bible,* and *Other Commentaries* references are also used. If convicted by the Holy Spirit concerning any area of our life, remember, "*In whom we have redemption through His blood, even the forgiveness of sins:*" Colossians 1:14. Pray and ask for the Lord's mercy, forgiveness and help to overcome any problems, misunderstandings or blame. Each woman should be able to ask trusted Christian women to pray for them. They could ask for prayer from their husband, Christian friends and relatives or pastors and others in their church. The point is that prayer is essential, and trust is needed.

Where should we meet for this Study?

Teachers, it is important to note that many of these lessons can become very lengthy due to the conversations they spark, especially, when done in a small group setting. They should be taught one word per session, with the introduction and first lesson taught together. It is important to note that this study of the Titus 2 Woman is a 'teaching' ministry, so a Sunday School classroom would be a suitable location. Or it could be taught at a home. For large groups, conversation would be limited but an overall introduction to the subject, with smaller groups to meet later, might be profitable. Pray before and after each lesson.

These lessons are for the both the Aged Women and Young Women

Introduction, The Aged Woman

These lessons are for Aged Christian Women (or Young Women)

Behavior as Becometh Holiness, Not False Accusers, Not Given to Much Wine, Teachers of Good Things

The following lessons are for Young Christian Women
(and Aged Women to Learn and to Teach)

To Teach the Young Women, To Be Sober, To Love Your Husband, To Love Your Children, To Be Discreet, To Be Chaste, Keepers at Home, Good, Obedient to Their Own Husband, That the Word of God Be Not Blasphemed

Young women do not need to be taught the traits of the aged woman. However, most of the information being taught is meant for all Christians anyway. Presenting knowledge of something to look forward to and prepare for in their future is good. The Aged Women lessons can also be taught at the end of the teaching series. Pray and keep in mind *"All scripture is given by inspiration God, and is profitable for doctrine, for reproof, for correction, for instruction in righteousness:"* 2 Timothy 3:16 Teachers should try to teach at the age level of those being taught. However, always include the scriptures to back up the teaching no matter what age, so they know it comes from God.

Jesus died on the cross for us and Satan cringed. Satan won't like us getting to know our Savior and His word better. Or that we become closer and give each other strength. We should all pray for the Lord's protection from Satan's devices. We must not live in the enemy's camp. These lessons and our fellowship can help us avoid those wicked devices and the fiery darts of the devil. He knows he has lost the war, let's not let him win little battles.

Are women the only persons addressed in Titus 2?

God has given the Christian woman a responsibility in Titus 2 but He also gave instructions to the Christian preacher, Christian aged *men* and others in this book of the Bible. Speaking to preachers He said, *"But speak thou the things which become sound doctrine: That the aged men be sober, grave, temperate, sound in faith, in charity, in patience".* Titus 2:1,2 Read all of Titus 2.

For a short word study of Titus 2:1,2 see the following verses:

Things	1 Peter 4:7–11
Sound Doctrine	1 Timothy 1:9,10
Aged	2 Samuel 19:32, Job 29:8, Job 32:9
Sober	2 Corinthians 5:13 Definition of Sober: Strong's Concordance states as; Strong, Valiant (Sober in this verse is a different Greek word than for women's instruction in Titus to be Sober.)
Grave	1 Timothy 3:8 Definition of Grave: requiring serious thought, dignified, solemn *Solemn* means religious, serious, deeply earnest, rousing feelings of awe, being very impressive
Faith	Romans 4:5

A Prayer to Begin

Dear Heavenly Father and Our Lord Jesus Christ,

Thank you for being a God of forgiveness and grace. Thank you for your word, which you hold higher than even your name. It is a help and comfort to us, giving us guidance, knowledge, and wisdom for all time. Thank you, Lord, for the women who have so graciously offered their questions and advice in these lessons, bless them, Lord. And may these lessons be an encouragement to your women, enhancing lives and furthering our walk into your kingdom to be with you forevermore. Thank you for your Holy Spirit moving and guiding the lessons and encouraging a wave of love from you throughout your people. All glory and honor to you Lord. In Jesus name we pray. Amen

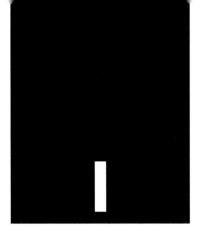

THE AGED WOMEN

Women are referred to as every member of the female gender. Every mother, daughter, sister, and female child can be categorized as women. The first woman, Eve, is the creation of God. Eve was created for the man, Adam. As the creation of God women are naturally capable upon maturity, together with the man, to procreate and bear children. As we search through the scriptures below, we allow them to define the meaning of the aged. The aged is younger than the very aged and older than the young. And the aged is not a child.

A. The Age of the Aged

1. How do each of the following verses describe the very aged and the aged?

   2 Samuel 19:32 "*Now Barzillai was a very aged man, even fourscore years old:*" (eighty years)

   Job 15:10 "*With us are both the gray headed and very aged men, much elder than thy father.*" Eliphaz the Temanite said this to Job. Notice he called out both the gray headed men and the very aged separately.

2. What did Elihu call Job and his friends in Job 32:6?

   Very old. Elihu was said to be a *young* man. There are commentaries that say Job was seventy years old, that would make him *aged,* but no reference is given to how they determined that.

3. According to Job what attitude do the *young* and *aged* in Job 29:8 have towards him?

   "*The young men saw me, and hid themselves: and the aged arose, and stood up.*"

   Did Job consider himself aged or very aged?

   It seems he considered himself *very aged*, by this statement.

This study is not about any one person. It is about GOD and His plan for His women. Remember God's forgiveness, truth, and grace is in His Son!

4. What was Paul called in Philemon Verse 9 when research shows he was approximately sixty years old when he authored the book of Philemon?

   Aged

B. The aged is a phrase used often in scriptures and when searching through the scriptures it is meant as older than the young (new or youthful).

1. Jesus is said to be a *young* child in Matthew 2:13–15. Herod slew all children two years old and under in an attempt to kill Jesus. How old would Jesus have been?

   About two years old

2. How old was Jesus when His family went to the Passover feast in Luke 2:42–43?

   Twelve years old

3. What was He called?

   A child

4. How old was Joseph in Genesis 37:2?

   Seventeen years old

5. How long had Joseph been in prison according to the verse in Genesis 41:1?

   Two years

6. In Genesis 41:12 what age was Joseph considered?

   A *young* man; nineteen years old

C. Summary of the aged and the young

1. Could we conclude that a *very aged* person is over eighty years old, and an *aged* person might have gray hair, but is sixty years old?

   Yes, according to this study but *Aged* could also be younger than that.

2. Does the reference to the word '*child*' mean that a child is between two years old and at least twelve years old? Yes

   And a young person beginning about seventeen to nineteen years of age? Yes

   Further study of a 'child' or 'lad' as Ishmael is described is found in Genesis 17:20,25, 21:6–21. According to Strong's Concordance, a 'damsel' as spoken of in many verses of the Bible; is a young woman, a virgin, an engaged girl.

3. Should we teach only married young women and those of legal age to be married the Titus 2 Woman? Of childbearing age?

    It could be before that for preparation

4. Define your own age by circling the appropriate age group.

    A child, young, aged, very aged

5. Have you been or will you be in a different age category?

    Yes, most likely.

6. What does the Bible say about the age and requirements to serve the Lord?

    Hebrews 7:1,2 says Jesus is our High Priest after the order of Melchizedek. Melchizedek's story is in Genesis 14:18. We teachers also need to prepare ourselves for our roles in God's plan for us. It is pleasing to our High Priest, Jesus. In Numbers 8, God instructed Moses to tell Aaron to have the Levites purify themselves for the Levitical Priesthood and then, in verses 24–26,

    "This is it that belongeth unto the Levites: from twenty and five years old and upward they shall go in to wait upon the service of the tabernacle of the congregation: and from the age of fifty years they shall cease waiting upon the service thereof, and shall serve no more: but shall minister with their brethren in the tabernacle of the congregation, to keep the charge, and shall do no service. Thus shalt thou do unto the Levites touching their charge."

7. Should being *spiritually aged* be a consideration for teaching about the Titus 2 Woman? That would mean being saved for about twenty years.

    It would be helpful for knowledge and wisdom's sake, but not necessarily.

8. Studies show a woman's childbearing age is fifteen to forty-four, but for health purposes the best ages for childbearing are twenty to thirty-five years of age. Does an aged woman need to be married or have children to teach Titus 2 Woman?

    No. These verses do not specify that is necessary.

9. Can we teach if we do not fall into the age categories we learned?

    Our study does not conclude that a very aged person should stop teaching or stop being a godly person or that a young person under twenty-five should not teach or be a godly person. But that *aged* women should do everything in accordance with Gods plan. God's word will prevail and accomplish its purpose.

    "So shall my word be that goeth forth out of my mouth: it shall not return unto me void, but it shall accomplish that which I please, and it shall prosper in the thing whereto I sent it." Isaiah 55:11

The Old Testament Proverbs 31 woman lives a diligent life: pleasing to her husband and family. The The New Testament Titus 2 woman has an even higher calling to teach young women, pleasing God by sharing her wisdom and gifts with younger Christian women.

10. What does Psalms 90:12 say God wants us to learn?

"So teach us to number our days, that we might apply our hearts unto wisdom."

Biblical Example of the Aged Woman: Find Anna in Luke 2:36–38

Anna was married for seven years and then was widowed. She was a prophetess and remained a widow living in the temple serving God. After Anna had served for eighty-four years, Mary and Joseph brought the baby Jesus to the temple. Anna gave thanks and spoke of Him to everyone who was looking for the Messiah and His redemption.

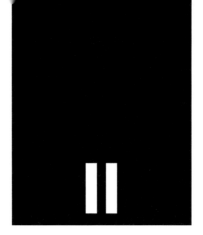

BEHAVIOR AS BECOMETH HOLINESS

Holiness is a condition which is suited to a sacred, reverent character and set apart to God. Holiness is the high standard of God which Jesus fulfilled. He will accomplish holiness in us. This is not to say we feel we have yet attained holiness but that we have faith in Him to accomplish holiness in us. It could take a lifetime, but it will happen when believers meet Him in person. Jesus is the author and finisher of our faith. Our faith in Him is what inspires us to want to be holy. *"But ye, beloved, building up yourselves on your most holy faith, praying in the Holy Ghost, keep yourselves in the love of God, looking for the mercy of our Lord Jesus Christ unto eternal life."* **Jude 1:20,21**

Gideon and his army surrounded the Midianite camp. They held pots in their hands, with lamps lit inside of them. As Gideon and his company broke the pots, they sounded their trumpets and called out, *"The sword of the LORD, and of Gideon."* The noise and the light from the lamps shining in quick succession scared their enemies and they ran away. This story is in Judges 7. As for us, we are like the clay pot. In Isaiah 64:8 the Bible says He is the potter, and we are the clay. As our bodies break down, like the pots in Gideon's story, God's holiness can shine through us. That day star arising in our hearts will shine beams of His light through us and our sounding out His wise word to those around us, will cause enemies to run away. All Christians and especially baby Christians can have hope to be a light in this world. Because His Word is a *"…lamp unto my feet, and a light unto my path."* **Psalm 119:105.** We can allow His word to guide us and lead us toward holiness. Haven't we all known a person who just shines and smiles even when in pain? Maybe a grandmother or elderly woman who exemplifies Christ. One who has scared us a little bit with her godly wisdom, putting fear of the Lord in us when we do the wrong thing. We know she is right, and it is for our own good, unless we are living in the enemy's camp. The Lord should win this battle for our hearts, not Satan.

A. Attaining Holiness

1. What does 2 Corinthians 7:1 say we should do to perfect holiness in ourselves?

   "Having therefore these promises, dearly beloved, let us cleanse ourselves from all filthiness of the flesh and spirit, perfecting holiness in the fear of God."

This study is not about any one person. It is about GOD and His plan for His women. Remember God's forgiveness, truth, and grace is in His Son!

2. Is the Lord going to help us to be holy? See 1 Thessalonians 3:13.

   "To the end he may stablish your hearts unblameable in holiness before God, even our Father, at the coming of our Lord Jesus Christ with all his saints."

3. What is the goal of holiness 2 Peter 1:3–4?

   "That by these you might be partakers of the divine nature,…"

4. What is to arise in our hearts according to 2 Peter 1:19?

   The day star

5. When will this be complete?

   Until the day dawn

6. What did Gideon and his men put into pitchers in Judges 7:16?

   Lamps

7. What happened when they broke the pitchers? Read Judges 7:20–21

   The lamps shined and drove away the enemy

8. What is God's word referred to in Psalms 119:105?

   A lamp

B. Behavior in this verse is our demeanor, our actions, our life, our walk, and our talk.

1. What kind of behavior did Paul avoid in 2 Thessalonians 3:7,8?

   "For yourselves know how ye ought to follow us: for we behaved not ourselves disorderly among you; Neither did we eat any man's bread for nought; but wrought with labour and travail night and day, that we might not be chargeable to any of you:"

2. How are we to behave according to Ephesians 5:8–12? Fill in the blanks.

   "For ye were sometimes darkness, but now are ye light in the Lord: ___walk___ as children of ___light___ : (For the fruit of the Spirit is in all ___goodness___ and ___righteousness___ and ___truth___ ;) Proving what is ___acceptable___ unto the Lord. And have no fellowship with the unfruitful works of darkness, but rather ___reprove___ them. For it is a ___shame___ even to ___speak___ of those things which are done of them in ___secret___ ."

   Reprove is to admonish, convince, convict, tell a fault, rebuke.

3. What does 1 Peter 4:15 say we should not suffer as?

"But let none of you suffer as a murderer, or as a thief, or as an evil doer, or as a busy body in other men's matters."

4. What human behavior traits are we to *stop* doing, as requested in the following verses?

    Colossians 3:5

    - stop fornication, mortify your members to do this
    - uncleanness
    - inordinate affection, meaning lacking restraint, (example: a woman chases after a man who does not return her affection, and a restraining order is issued against her), not using moderation
    - evil concupiscence, meaning strong, evil, or abnormal desire
    - covetousness (which is idolatry)

    Colossians 3:8,9

    - anger
    - wrath
    - malice, meaning active ill will or evil intent
    - blasphemy (saying things against God)
    - filthy communication
    - lying to one another (telling falsehoods)

5. What godly behavior traits are we encouraged to *apply* to our lives, as shown in the following verses?

    Colossians 3:12,13

    - bowels of mercy
    - kindness
    - humbleness of mind
    - meekness, meaning not inclined to anger, gentle; Webster also defines as, spineless! (Our Example: Jesus had no guile meaning He was candid and frank, not spineless, telling the truth, in love!)
    - longsuffering, meaning patience
    - forbearance, meaning to put up with
    - forgiveness

    Colossians 3:14–17

    - Put on charity.
    - Let the peace of God rule in your heart.
    - Let the Word of Christ dwell in you richly, in all wisdom.
    - Teach and admonish one another in psalms, hymns, and spiritual songs.
    - Sing with grace in your hearts to the Lord.
    - Do all in the name of the Lord Jesus, giving thanks to God.

C. Summary

1. Are there things in our behavior that need to change because of what we learned in this study?

    All of us do. But these can remain personal between you and God. Be patient and pray and remember our salvation in Christ . Teach with love, grace, and forgiveness, not risking the law versus grace!

2. Is this living under the law instead of grace?

    Teaching holiness can risk law versus grace we must always remember salvation through faith. Faith is the place where we all begin. It is our faith that pleases God, see Hebrews 11:6. Romans 6:14–15 says, *"For sin shall not have dominion over you: for ye are not under the law but under grace. What then? Shall we sin, because we are not under the law, but under grace? God forbid."*

3. Does daily prayer and Bible study help to accomplish holiness in our life? See Ephesians 5:26–27

    "That he might sanctify and cleanse it with the washing of water by the word, That he might present it to himself a glorious church, not having spot, or wrinkle, or any such thing; but that it should be holy and without blemish." The 'it' in verse twenty-six is 'us' the church. People need to be in church to hear the word, *"So then faith cometh by hearing and hearing by the Word of God."* Romans 10:17 Hearing the word accomplishes the washing of us. As we hear His word and we grow in our faith in Him, we can gain confidence in overcoming our sins and doubts even our addictions, and that is the washing. Philippians 1:6 says, *"being confident of this very thing, that he which hath begun a good work in you will perform it until the day of Jesus Christ:"* People have searched the Bible time and again to try to prove they are going to hell but only find His mercy, love, grace, and forgiveness.

Biblical Example of Being in Behavior as Becometh Holiness:
Find Leah in Genesis 29–35, 46:15 & 49:31.

Jacob loved Rachel. However, it was his first wife, Leah, who was also Rachel's sister, that followed him, accepted his ways, and accepted his God. Rachel, brought along her idols after she too had married Jacob. Leah bore Jacob six sons, who were six of the twelve tribes of Israel. It is to her honor God chose her son Judah's lineage to bring Jesus into the world. In death, she lies in the cave at Mamre next to Jacob's side along with the other Patriarchs in the family, Abraham and Sarah, and Isaac and Rebekah. Rachel was buried elsewhere. A conclusion from this historical account could be that a man should marry the woman who loves him the most.

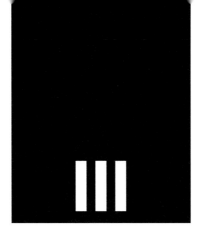

NOT FALSE ACCUSERS

There might have been a person who has falsely accused us or lied about us or someone that we know. It is troubling. A misunderstanding of something we said or did might have been an excuse for their false accusations. Or there might be some behavior or personality trait they just didn't like about us which might be totally unintentional on our part. But this person just had to twist it to what they think is to their advantage. Going about telling everyone around them their innuendos and lies. Some people do this intentionally to hurt us. They want to try to destroy us and our reputations. Gossip and lies seem to be part of their makeup. However, this should not be part of the Christian woman or any Christian. If any of us have been drawn into falsely accusing or lying, or believing those lies, know that God is not pleased with that. And we should ask for forgiveness and stop this behavior.

A. False is a lie, a lie is not the truth, to say falsely, to calculate to deceive. Satan is the father of lies.

1. Who does 2 Corinthians 11:31 say knows whether we lie or not?

   "The God and father of our Lord Jesus Christ, which is blessed for evermore, knoweth that I lie not."

2. Who does John 8:44 say is the father of lies?

   Jesus speaking to Pharisees, *"Ye are of your father the devil, and the lusts of your father ye will do. He was a murderer from the beginning, and abode not in the truth, because there is no truth in him. When he speaketh a lie, he speaketh of his own: for he is a liar, and the father of it."*

3. Should a saved person stop lying? See Colossians 3:9.

   Yes. *"Lie not one to another, seeing that ye have put off the old man with his deeds;"*

This study is not about any one person. It is about GOD and His plan for His women. Remember God's forgiveness, truth, and grace is in His Son!

B. An accuser is a slanderer or those who find fault with the demeanor of others

That is, their manner toward others or the conduct of others. A slanderer is one who spreads their innuendos and criticisms in the church. An accuser or slanderer can destroy reputations.

1. Should we bring accusations against an elder in the church?

    "Rebuke not an elder, but intreat him as a father; and the younger men as brethren; The elder women as mothers; the younger as sisters, with all purity." See 1 Timothy 5:1,2

    To rebuke is to appeal to, call out, or strike with words.

2. How can we protect our elders from false accusers, according to 1 Timothy 5:19?

    "Against an elder receive not an accusation, but before two or three witnesses."

3. In Matthew 5:11 how does Jesus feel about a person when another has lied and accused them falsely?

    "Blessed are ye, when men shall revile you, and persecute you, and shall say all manner of evil against you falsely, for my sake."

4. 2 Timothy 3:1–7 warns Christians of false accusers and others that will come into the church. In verses 6 and 7 who they will lead away from the knowledge of the truth?

    "…silly women laden with sins, led away with divers lust, Everlearning, and never able to come to the knowledge of the truth:"

5. What about reputations? Do we sometimes make comments that might hurt or destroy a person's reputation before others?

    We need to be careful to watch what we say.

6. What are the three steps we should take according to Matt 18:15–20 when a person in the church trespasses against us?

    There is a process which is actually good to use for anyone, anywhere, that trespasses against us. Pray, then...

    1. Go talk to them alone of this issue. A woman should not be alone with a man to avoid any improprieties, ask your spouse or another Christian to speak to them. If they do not hear, then,

    2. Take one or two more witnesses, so every word will be established to them. If they still do not hear

    3. Tell it to the pastor of your church, he should use the discretion needed to tell it before the church.

C. Summary

1. What does Colossians 3:13 say I should do if a Christian lies to or falsely accuses us?

    "forbearing one another, and forgiving one another, if any man have a quarrel against any: even as Christ forgave you, so also do ye." Forbearing means to put up with one another.

2. What should I do if an unsaved person lies about us or falsely accuse us? See Mark 11:25

    "And when ye stand praying, forgive, if ye have ought against any: that your Father also which is in heaven may forgive you your trespasses".

3. What should be the first step to do for a person who falsely accuses or trespasses against us?

    Pray for God to restore them in truth, forgiveness, and grace.

4. How can we confront ourselves of the warning to not be false accusers? 1 John 1:9

    "If we confess our sins, he is faithful and just to forgive us our sins, and to cleanse us from all unrighteousness."

    Remember…Salvation through faith! Repent and walk away from the sins we have been convicted of!

Biblical Example of Not Being a False Accuser: Find Damaris in Acts 17:34

Damaris was a woman who was converted to Christianity through the preaching of Paul at Mars Hill in Athens. Paul was being mocked and falsely accused, because he spoke of the resurrection. She was one of the people who stood with him and was mentioned in the book of Acts.

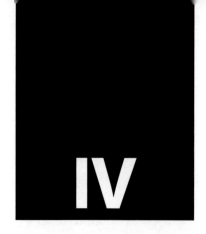

IV

NOT GIVEN TO MUCH WINE

Today in our society serving beverages containing alcohol seems to be commonplace. Wine is not for aged women to drink too much of, so we won't be in bondage to it and so our minds can be on Christ. Our society promotes many things that God is not pleased with and wants us to avoid, this lesson addresses only wine. The word 'wine' is from the Greek word *Oinos*. It's probably referring to the drink which has fermentation, which has turned into alcohol in content. However, there are scholars that believe the same Greek word was also used at times for non-fermented wine, which is grape juice. The topic of whether a person should drink fermented wine is not known to be a point of salvation in most Christian denominations. We are not to argue among ourselves about God's Word. And of course, we are told in the Bible not to get drunk or be given to strong drink. Christians have been called to abstain from strong drink, so we don't do something wicked or appear as wicked people. If anyone is convicted about drinking alcohol or if anyone is responsible for younger or weaker Christians, who might be in our homes or ministry, but especially if your church forbids it, then do not drink it.

A. For us to be given to something is to be enslaved to it or in bondage to it. 'Much' is the amount or degree of something; or a lot of something.

1. When a person is in bondage to something they are born after what? See Galatians 4:23

   "But he who was of the bondwoman was born after the flesh; but he of the freewoman was by promise". Keep in mind, *"His mercies are new every morning and his compassions fail not."* Lamentations 3:22–23

2. In Galatians 4:3–5 who redeemed us from bondage?

   "Even so we, when we were children, were in bondage under the elements of the world: But when the fullness of the time was come, God sent forth his Son, made of a woman, made under the law, To redeem them that were under the law, that we might receive the adoption of sons." He sent His Son to redeem us from bondage.

This study is not about any one person. It is about GOD and His plan for His women. Remember God's forgiveness, truth, and grace is in His Son!

3. As Christian women can we overcome bondage? See Galatians 5:1

    "Stand fast therefore in the liberty wherewith Christ hath made us free, and be not entangled again with the yoke of bondage."

    Pray about it and ask for help, if needed. People including Christians are held in bondage to many things God has not meant for them to be in bondage to. These bondages get in the way of His plan for us. With a sincere desire to please God and with His help these obstacles can be overcome by us. We should pray for each other to overcome any bondage that our fellow Christians cannot overcome on their own.

B. Why not drink 'too much wine' ?

1. Why does Romans 14:21 say we should not drink too much wine?

    "It is good neither to eat flesh, nor to drink wine, nor any thing whereby thy brother stumbleth, or is offended, or is made weak."

2. What does Proverbs 20:1 say about a person who is deceived by wine?

    "Wine is a mocker, strong drink is raging: and whosoever is deceived thereby is not wise."

3. In Proverbs 23:20,21 who is to be avoided?

    "Be not among winebibbers; among riotous eaters of flesh:"

    Winebibbers are those given to, too much wine. Riotous means no restraint.

    And who shall come to poverty? Impoverished spiritually and economically.

    "For the drunkard and the glutton shall come to poverty: and drowsiness shall clothe a man with rags."

4. What does God's word say about wine in Proverbs 31:4–7?

    It is not for kings, or they might forget Gods law. It is meant for those that be of heavy hearts. In the past wine was also used for medicinal purposes.

5. Did the marriage feast in John 2 meet any of the criteria of Proverbs 31:4–7?

    No, a marriage is a joyous occasion.

6. According to John 1 Jesus is the Word of God. Ask yourself if Jesus would make more alcohol for people at the end of the marriage feast found in John 2?

    This is debatable. Most scholars believe it was the drink with alcohol that Jesus made, but some do not. His time for miracles had not yet come but He did it, to please His mother, Mary.

C. Summary

1. Would it have been more difficult in biblical times to avoid drinking too much wine?

   Probably. Water was a precious commodity especially in smaller towns, so they drank wine instead. Water travelled to Jerusalem down the mountains in cement like trenches. It was not always abundant.

2. Has your church asked members to not drink alcohol? See your church charter and bylaws. Teachers should take special precautions. Romans 14:21

   "It is good neither to eat flesh, nor to drink wine, nor any thing whereby thy brother stumbleth, or is offended, or is made weak." Also read Daniel 1:3–21, it shows that Daniel chose water over wine.

3. If we know a Christian woman who is 'given to much wine' what should we do? See Galatians 6:1

   "Brethren, if a man be overtaken in a fault, ye which are spiritual, restore such an one in the spirit of meekness; considering thyself, lest thou also be tempted."

   When a person is in a spiritual battle, and the wicked are throwing their fiery darts, that person may retreat to dress their own wounds. It is then that a stronger Christian could come to them and help restore them to the grace of God. Knowing God's love through these difficult times can help grow their shield of faith for the future.

Biblical Example of Not being Given to Much Wine: Find Mary, the mother of Jesus, in the Gospels of Matthew, Luke, John, Acts.

God chose Mary to bring His son into the world. Her quotes were, *"And Mary said, my soul doth magnify the Lord,"* in Luke 1:46. Another quote Mary spoke was about Jesus to the servants at the wedding feast, *"… Whatsoever he saith, do it ."* John 2:5 She had been told there was no more wine, and she urged Jesus to perform a miracle to produce more wine. Her words are a good lesson for us all, whatever Jesus says, *do it*! The wine made was most likely fermented becoming alcohol. Some people say it is questionable that Mary, the mother of Jesus, would condone the making of fermented wine for possible drunkenness at the end of the marriage feast. But Jesus did make the wine and the ruler of the feast said the wine was the best, whether it was alcohol or not.

HAVE THESE LESSONS BEEN HARD?

Take heart. We are not alone in feeling scared or ashamed of the way we have behaved in our lives. There are very evident acts of sin and then there are those internal sins that God reveals to us. They all usually manifest in anger or other misbehavior. Miss Charlotte Elliott was born in the late 1700's in England. Through her struggles, and the anger they produced, she eventually found that Jesus alone would give her the courage and strength to live her life, as an invalid. After being saved, and for the rest of her life, she used her talents for Jesus, authoring books and hymns. Charlotte wrote the words to the famous hymn, "Just As I Am." Once she had truly accepted Jesus she began to exemplify and glorify Christ. Even if we have been saved for a while and the lessons we learn or will learn from God's word are hard for us. Remember to come to Him *just as we are*. Confess our sins and He will forgive us and cleanse us from all unrighteousness. See 1 John 1:9 [1]

---

[1] Note 1: "JUST AS I AM" by Charlotte Elliott is a song of Surrender that could be sung at this point. It would be a powerful addition to this teaching. For the tune and stanza's, see a Hymnal or try to find it on the Internet. Also, find other books and hymns and the life story of Charlotte on the Internet or a Library.

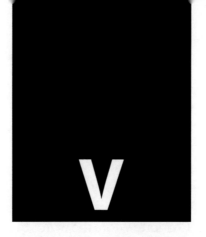

TEACHERS OF GOOD THINGS

According to Strong's Concordance, the Greek word for 'teachers' is *Numphon*; meaning from the bridal room; bride chamber. The author, the Apostle Paul, used the word *numphon*, a reminder that we, the church, are the bride of Christ. As such we should teach with love and knowledge of Him. That is the purpose of this ministry. As His representatives on earth we should teach the good things we receive from Him. First, we need to get with Him in the Bridal Chamber. We are in His "bridal chamber" when we are studying His word and having prayer time with Him. It is there that Jesus will reveal those things He wants to teach us. It is important to note that He will never contradict His word and knowing His word protects us from contradicting His teachings.

A. **A teacher is a person who trains, one who causes others to learn.**

1. Why should we study before we teach?

   "Study to shew thyself approved unto God, a workman that needeth not to be ashamed, rightly dividing the word of truth." 2 Timothy 2:15

2. What place do teachers have in the church, as outlined in 1 Corinthians 12:28?

   "And God hath set some in the church, first apostles, secondarily prophets, thirdly teachers, after that miracles, then gifts of healings, helps, governments, diversities of tongues."

3. In Romans 12:4–8 what is the position of teaching?

   It is an office we hold as <u>a part</u> of the one body of Christ, verse 4 states, *"For as we have many members in one body, and all members have not the same office;"*

4. According to Ephesians 4:15–16 how should we teach?

   "But speaking the truth in love, may grow up into him in all things, which is the head, even Christ: From whom the whole body fitly joined together and compacted by that which every joint supplieth, according to the effectual working in the measure of every part, maketh increase of the body unto the edifying of itself in love."

This study is not about any one person. It is about GOD and His plan for His women. Remember God's forgiveness, truth, and grace is in His Son!

5. Why should we teach?

If we do not teach the church could become crippled, as we currently see happening. Our sisters are left with no direction or Christian goals and easily sifted by Satan. But Jesus, alone, can help bring the church back to health and keep it healthy.

6. In Titus 2 should all Christian women someday be teachers? See 1 Peter 5:1–4.

Aged women, as directed by the Word and the Holy Spirit

"The elders which are among you I exhort, who am also an elder, and a witness of the suffering of Christ, and also a partaker of the glory that shall be revealed: Feed the flock of God which is among you, taking the oversight thereof, not by constraint, but willingly; not for filthy lucre, but of a ready mind; Neither as being lords over God's heritage, but being ensamples to the flock. And when the chief Shepherd shall appear, ye shall receive a crown of glory that fadeth not away."

B. Good is what is morally honorable, pleasing to God, beneficial.

1. What does Jesus say in Matthew 19:17 about who is good?

"And he said unto him, Why callest thou me good? there is none good but one, that is, God: but if thou wilt enter into life, keep the commandments." (i.e., love God, love others)

2. An example of being teachers of good things is in Philemon 6:

Why? *"That the communication of thy faith may become effectual…"*

How? *"…by the acknowledging of every good thing which is in you in Christ Jesus."*

3. How can the fruits of the Spirit help aged women teach younger women? Read Galatians 5:22–26

"But the fruit of the Spirit is love, joy, peace, longsuffering, gentleness, goodness, faith, meekness, temperance: against such there is no law. And they that are Christ's have crucified the flesh with the affections and lusts. If we live in the Spirit, let us also walk in the Spirit. Let us not be desirous of vain glory, provoking one another, envying one another."

Vain glory, provoking, envying…let us pray to never, ever, let these be our goals but to only do the will of the Lord and please Him. See also 1 Thessalonians 2

C. Summary

Give examples of aged women showing young women in the church their willingness to help them learn the traits in the Titus 2 Woman ministry. These suggestions are from godly women, during their study of this lesson.

- Seek them out, greet them at the door, speak to them of their family, job, make them feel welcome and comfortable.

- Provide a time and place at the church to meet for bible study so women can be taught from the Titus 2 woman's ministry, a classroom or small group setting might be the most beneficial. Presenting it in a large group might work so some women do not feel left out but smaller groups allow for more personal growth. Or you can teach one on one or even in general conversation which could spark an interest in knowing more.
- Try to include any born-again Christian woman.

Pray now...that all Christian women walk together, and work together, in the household of faith...FOR HIS GLORY!

Biblical Example of Teachers of Good Things: Find Euodias in Philippians 4:2,3

Euodias was a leader of teaching other women in the church at Philippi. She had labored with Paul in the gospel. The Apostle Paul told Euodias to be *of the same mind in the Lord* as Syntyche. Syntyche was another woman in the church who could also have been a teacher of women and had also labored with Paul in the gospel. It is apparent that Paul addressed the two women because they either had different opinions or were struggling in their relationship. They must have taken Paul's advice and made amends because they were not mentioned again. Paul stated that both their names were written in the Book of Life. Praise the Lord, we will meet them also. We too need to be of the same mind in the Lord and not let friction separate us. "*Can two walk together, except they be agreed?*" Amos 3:3

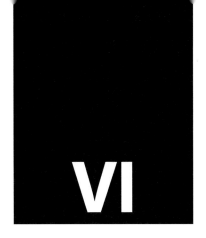

VI

TO TEACH THE YOUNG WOMEN

To teach is to train. The Strong's Concordance gives the Greek word *rhipizo* for the word teach in this passage. It means to fan, bellows, breeze up, agitate into waves. Jamieson-Fausset Brown says that aged women were to school the young women, so Titus did not have too. According to John Wesley's Notes, Timothy was to instruct the young women himself, but not Titus. Although, in 1 Timothy 4:12 Paul tells Timothy to "*Let no man despise thy youth;*" Wesley might have evidence that Timothy was not as young as Titus when teaching women. Also, the aged women in the book of Timothy might have been baby Christians only teaching the law, and not grace (see 1 Timothy 1:5–8). So, it is evident Paul trusted Timothy to teach the women. Or his mother and grandmother; Lois, and Eunice, were there taking on that role or at least monitoring him as he interacted with the young women. The Apostle Paul does not specify why Timothy was to teach and Titus was to have aged women teach the young women.

A. Being trained

1. Should all Christian women ask for and seek those qualities of the aged women in Titus 2:3?

   Paul does not specify that some women should not seek those qualities. We know God's plan is that we should all be seeking to "*be in behavior as becometh holiness, not false accusers, not given to much wine, teachers of good things.*" See 2 Timothy 2:24,25

   "*And the servant of the Lord must not strive; but be gentle unto all men, apt to teach, patient; in meekness instructing those that oppose themselves; if God peradventure will give them repentance to the acknowledging of the truth;*"

2. Should we be trained in the qualities outlined because they do not come naturally to us?

   Maybe.

This study is not about any one person. It is about GOD and His plan for His women. Remember God's forgiveness, truth, and grace is in His Son!

3. Are we to be trained by other women because we are the weaker vessel and need to be strengthened together? See 1 Peter 3:7

   Yes.

   "Likewise, ye husbands, dwell with them according to knowledge, giving honour unto the wife, as unto the weaker vessel, and as being heirs together of the grace of life; that your prayers be not hindered."

4. Old Testament women worshipped in a separate place from the men. They were allowed on the mezzanine or top floor of the temple. Who does 1 Timothy 2:11 & 12 say we are not to teach?

   "Let the woman learn in silence with all subjection. But I suffer not a woman to teach, nor to usurp authority over the man, but to be in silence."

   Silence in the church; when men are preaching or teaching unless they ask for questions or answers to their questions.

5. Please consider that in any occupation a certain amount of time, energy and resources are spent to become 'trained' in that field. Should a younger woman or new Christian be willing to be 'trained'? 1 Peter 5:5–7

   "Likewise, ye younger, submit yourselves unto the elder. Yea, all of you be subject one to another, and be clothed with humility: for God resisteth the proud, and giveth grace to the humble. Humble yourselves therefore under the mighty hand of God, that he may exalt you in due time; Casting all your care upon him; for he careth for you."

6. Should an aged or older Christian woman be willing to help train the younger women? 1 Peter 5:8–11

   Hopefully, for all our sakes, we need to…

   "Be sober, be vigilant; because your adversary the devil, as a roaring lion, walketh about, seeking whom he may devour, Whom resist stedfast in the faith, knowing that the same afflictions are accomplished in your brethren that are in the world. But the God of all grace, who hath called us unto his eternal glory by Christ Jesus, after that ye have suffered a while, make you perfect, stablish, strengthen, settle you."

   Illness, temptation, sin, and troubles come to us all. We will all suffer these things in some way.

7. Some misconceptions of women concerning the Titus 2 woman is that they are to be babysitters, cook and clean for younger women or always work the nursery. Although those are good ministries, they are not what the Titus 2 Woman ministry is about. This is a teaching ministry. What are some reasons why aged women do not teach the young women? These suggestions are from godly women, during their study of this lesson.

Too busy	Lack of knowledge
Fearful the young women already know it all	Secret sin or don't feel holy enough
It is not their responsibility	Lack of trust in sharing themselves

It is not their daughter

Don't think it is necessary

Don't believe God will use them

Lack of belief in themselves

Because no one taught them

8. Why should the aged women teach younger women? These suggestions are from godly women, during their study of this lesson.

Women are the weaker vessel and need truth

Women need support and encouragement

To stay young at heart

Because the book of Titus tells women too

To bridge the age divide and any divide

For developing love and faith unfeigned

(like Lois and Eunice, Timothy's mother, and grandmother)

Biblical Example of a Teacher of Young Women: Find Mary Magdalene in Matthew 27:56,61 28:1, Mark 15:40,47 16:1–19 Luke 8:2, 24:10 John 19:25 20:1–18.

After her healing from seven demons making her seem insane. Magdalene appears as one of the most devoted women of the Bible. Eight times Mary Magdalene is mentioned in connection with other women. Her love of Christ and service to Him speaks of a woman appreciating her salvation and the love of God that came with it. Joanna and Susanna were also women healed by Christ of evil spirits. His salvation is sure, but it is our willingness to allow Him to work in us that makes us into the person God had in mind for us to be to begin with.

"Wherefore I say unto thee, Her sins, which are many, are forgiven; for she loved much: but to whom little is forgiven, the same loveth little." Luke 7:47

TO BE SOBER

To be sober is to use self-control. Also, to have mental and emotional balance. To be serious (about God), sparing in use, listening to the inner voice, and choosing to do what would most glorify God. Christian behavior sets us apart from the world. Being sober is a self-restraint or bodily action that should govern all our passions and desires and help enable believers to be conformed to the image of Christ. *Being sober is to think and act!*

A. Sober Defined

Strong's Concordance notes the Greek word for Sober is *Sophronizo*; to make of sound mind, discipline or correct. To teach discipline and help correct behavior or dress. Vine's Dictionary says being sober, is to teach or train and cultivate sound judgment and prudence. Webster's Dictionary states sober has five different meanings. 1. To not be drunk; 2. To be serious or grave; 3. Plain or subdued; without frivolity or excess or exaggeration, 4. Rational or impartial, 5. Abstemious or temperate. Abstemious means moderate, abstain from, holding back on indulgence. Prudence is consideration and understanding or planning *before* action and will be addressed in another lesson.

B. Sober, Biblical Application

Matthew Henry's Commentary states that being sober and discreet in Titus 2 is so young women will not expose themselves to fatal temptations that at first might seem to be a want of discretion or lack of understanding.

1. Who seeks to devour us if we are not sober? See 1 Peter 5:8

   "*Be sober, be vigilant; because your adversary the devil, as a roaring lion, walketh about, seeking whom he may devour.*"

2. Is there a reason we should be sober for our future? See 1 Peter 1:13

   "*Wherefore gird up the loins of your mind, be sober, and hope to the end for the grace that is to be brought unto you at the revelation of Jesus Christ;*"

This study is not about any one person. It is about GOD and His plan for His women. Remember God's forgiveness, truth, and grace is in His Son!

3. Should we ask ourselves in every action and thought and word, "Does it please God"?

    Yes.

C. Being Sober in Dress

One issue of being sober is our choice of dress. We are to be modest, letting our heart be our adorning, and avoid looking evil. It is important for young women to know that older Christian women want to help them see God's plan for them and this study group is not the place for judgement. The God given traits discussed in these lessons are for our benefit and accomplishing these traits is pleasing to God. Being sober has kept women throughout history from the heartaches and regrets of not following God's plan for us. Not being sober has made Christian women to be mistaken for someone they are not. See footnote on the first page of each section. What guidelines for the way we dress, are given in the following verses?

> 1 Timothy 2:9,10?

> *"In like manner also, that women adorn themselves in modest apparel, with shamefacedness and sobriety; not with broided hair, or gold, or pearls, or costly array; but (which becometh women professing godliness) with good works."*

> Strong's Concordance definition for *Shamefacedness* is modest, awe toward God, the idea of downcast eyes; Broided is the intertwining of hair, plait or braid, adorn with ornaments. The Latin Vulgate suggests ringlets or curls. The idea of this passage is that the outward appearance is not what makes us beautiful, and we should look to our inner being for true beauty.

> 1 Peter 3:3,4 *"Whose adorning let it not be that outward adorning of plaiting the hair, and of wearing of gold, or of putting on of apparel; But let it be the hidden man of the heart, in that which is not corruptible even the ornament of a meek and quiet spirit, which is in the sight of God of great price."*

> 1 Thessalonians 5:22 *"Abstain from all appearance of evil"*.

> The way we dress can make us appear as something we are not.

4. Why should we care about our dress?

    God wants us to represent Him. A new Christian or one that is unfamiliar with God's specific teaching on how we dress might not like this teaching and might feel uncomfortable with their dress. Discussion might ignite questions about I Cor 9: 20–23. Paul states that he became *as they are* in order to save or gain some. Verse 22 specifically states that Paul had a single focus for doing that and it was to win others to Christ. This idea can be an excuse to try to be or dress like the world. We should examine our motives and asking why do we dress as we do? Are we dressing to be popular with a certain crowd? God knows our heart; He wants the best for us. Women might also question, isn't this legalistic telling us how to dress? John 7:24 says, "*Judge not according to the appearance, but judge righteous judgment.*" This teaching is from God's word.

5. How should we view being sober?

    To be sober is to act on or *do* what would most glorify God and not anyone else. Thinking through our choices and applying His word to our life is a heart issue. Consider if you want to please God and bring Him honor, honor to your family and church. Also, for good self-esteem in the future. He calls us to be modest which means not being bold or assertive in our dress and behavior. Placing a moderate estimate on one's ability or worth, being decent, and unpretentious. This manifests in not spending more on clothes than we can afford or dressing more extravagantly than a situation or event calls for. We are worth more to Jesus than our dress sometimes shows. He looks at our heart.

    Teachers, we need grace when addressing the issue of being sober, especially about dress. It might be advantageous to show pictures of different situations where someone dresses modestly, but stylish. And also pictures of immodest dress. Each woman will be at different stages of Christian growth so please do not compare the actual women in your study group or point them out whether for good taste or bad. Try not let others in the room do this either. God will judge their reaction to this teaching. To remedy our wardrobes, we can suggest taking it one step at a time as we buy new clothing. Being mindful of our choices in the meantime to try to accommodate modesty. Let the Holy Spirit do His work on each woman's heart. It is a wonderful thing when our will lines up with His will.

D. Making Sober Choices

We do have a choice about being sober.

1. Why are some women not choosing to be sober? These suggestions are from godly women as they studied this lesson.

They have no knowledge of God's plan for them	In dress, they want to be attractive or sexy, especially to men
They think they will not have fun	In dress, they want to be popular, in style, or 'cool'
They don't want to have to think things through all the time, they want to be spontaneous	They want to dress for the weather
They think others will make fun of them	They think they won't be comfortable

2. What benefits do we get from being sober? These suggestions are from godly women as they studied this lesson.

To keep from believing worldly standards, instead of God's	The joy of our salvation is not blocked from us
To have God's approval	Prevents future shame
To be in charge of myself, my body, my mind, my words	For future joy, with our husband, children, and grandchildren

    "…Looking unto Jesus the author and finisher of our faith; who for the joy that was set before him endured the cross, despising the shame, and set down at the right hand of the throne of God." Hebrews 12:2

3. What do Christian men think of women that are worldly? When asked about these things men may revert to sexual overtones and reveal that they might not be living up to God's expectations themselves. Men need grace and prayer also. If, women discover their spouse or boyfriend's mindset is not in alignment with God, they need to pray for them. Further discussion on God's direction might change their mind. These answers are from godly women's questions to their spouses while they studied this lesson. Ask your own fathers, husbands, boyfriends, friends.

They are immature	They cannot trust them
They make them feel uncomfortable	They need to look away and stay away from them
They are flighty	They twitter from one man to another
They avoid them, to avoid the appearance of evil	

4. What do Christian men think of women who are sober? These answers are from godly women's questions to their spouses while they studied this lesson. Ask your own fathers, husbands, boyfriends, friends.

They trust them	They would marry one
They respect them	They would give them the honor they deserve
They can be friends with them	

Biblical Example of being Sober: Find Lydia in Acts 16:12–15,40

Lydia was a Jewish businesswoman in Thyatira, she sold purple, which was a fashion material and sought-after color. It was a color used by wealthy people. Lydia worshipped God. When she met the apostle Paul on the beach and heard him speak, the Lord opened her heart to the gospel that Paul presented. After that, she and her whole household believed on Jesus, and they were baptized. She then offered her home for the use of Paul, the missionaries, and saints. Paul also went to her home after he was released from prison.

VIII

TO LOVE THEIR HUSBANDS

Webster says love implies an intense affectionate concern for another, a fondness or deep devotion or a deep and tender feeling. In the Greek language there are three words that are translated into English as the word 'love.' They are *Eros*, which means physical love. *Phileo* which is the friendship love, and *Agape* which is Godly love. *Agape* love according to the Strong's Concordance, is to love in a social or moral sense. All three types of love are welcomed into the marriage relationship. *Eros* is only undefiled in marriage. *Phileo* and *Agape* love are proper loves for children and others.

This study is a teaching tool for aged women to share their experience and to teach younger women to love. To love as God shows them from those moments in the bridal chamber with Him, which is the time spent in Bible study and prayer. Aged women should remember why they have been drawn to this ministry and continue in prayer about it. This lesson is meant for peace in the family and families of God. No matter how much we learn to love others, we must always remember, God loves them more! 'Love your Husband', in the Strong's Concordance shows the Greek word for love is *Philandros* or *philos* or *phileo* and means dear friend and fondness. In Vine's Dictionary it is said to mean tender affection, a friendship, a cherishing above all else, except God.

Let us cherish our husbands, and our friends for their good, not our own. Just as our Savior has instructed us in ways to live that are for our benefit.

A. Husband and Wife

1. In Genesis 2:18 why did the Lord God say He would make Adam a help meet?

   "And the LORD God said, It is not good that the man should be alone; I will make him an help meet for him."

2. The Lord God then formed Eve from Adam's rib which God took from his side. What then does Genesis 2:24 say that a man is to do because of this?

   "Therefore shall a man leave his father and his mother, and shall cleave unto his wife: and they shall be one flesh."

This study is not about any one person. It is about GOD and His plan for His women. Remember God's forgiveness, truth, and grace is in His Son!

Marriage was first established in the Garden of Eden. One woman for one man. Men also need to follow God's word. God made Eve from Adam's rib. This did not mean *all* men have one fewer rib than women, but God did use one of Adam's ribs in creating Eve.

3.   Proverbs 18:24 says *"A man that hath friends must shew himself friendly: and there is a friend that sticketh closer than a brother."* This teaching means that Christ sticks closer to us than a brother, should a woman also stick that close to her husband?

Yes, that is preferrable since woman was taken from Adams side and formed from his rib. Our husband is meant to be our dear friend; so, staying by his side is logical since married persons are to be one flesh. Why wouldn't we want to be best friends for life with our husband?

B. Our Souls, our Minds, our Friend

One definition from Vine's Dictionary of the 'soul' is the natural life of the invisible part of man.
The soul is also defined as the seat of the element in man in which he perceives, reflects, feels, and desires. A believer's thinking and emotions should first be toward God and His approval. When a husband and wife are alike in both mind and soul, they can be considered 'soul' mates. Along with an initial physical attraction this is the key to true love and to a marriage with fewer obstacles to face between you. So, both a husband and wife should think alike about God, feel alike in their emotions towards each other, and have a physical attraction to each other. This would also be a marriage that even a mother would approve of for their daughter. Knowing and resting in that she is safe in her husband's, and God's, love.

1.   How do we know the woman in the Song of Solomon 3:4 knows she loves the man she wants to marry?

"It was but a little that I passed from them, but I found him whom my soul loveth: I held him and would not let him go, until I had brought him into my mother's house, and into the chamber of her that conceived me."

The 'them' referred to are the watchmen. She loved him from her soul, which is not just a physical or heart issue. The soul is closely related to the mind and is a necessary element to friendship, thinking alike. And she wanted her mother to meet him. Women should take our love home to meet our mother. Not necessarily for him to take us home to meet his mother, as some people's tradition has been. He is supposed to leave and cleave according to Genesis 2:24.

2.   True righteousness begins in a believer who has first done what is right by believing God, who loved the world and sent His son, Jesus, to save us from our sins. Jesus told John the Baptist it was up to them; John and Jesus, to fulfill all righteousness regarding baptizing Jesus. A nonbeliever has not believed and cannot fulfill all righteousness. Jesus is the light of the world and a nonbeliever does not have that light. But there is hope in Jesus for them. So, knowing these truths, who shouldn't a Christian woman marry according to 2 Corinthians 6:14?

"Be ye not unequally yoked together with unbelievers: for what fellowship hath righteousness with unrighteousness? And what communion hath light with darkness?"

3. Proverbs 31:10–12 shows why the benefit of a virtuous wife is far above rubies, what are they?

   "Who can find a virtuous woman? For her price is far above rubies. The heart of her husband doth safely trust in her, so that he shall have no need of spoil."

   Virtue should result in a husband having no need for other sexual pursuits.

4. In Ephesians 5:27 why does Christ love His bride, the church (Read aloud, Ephesians 5:21–33)?

   "That he might present it to himself a glorious church, not having spot, or wrinkle, or any such thing: but that it should be holy and without blemish."

   Verse 33 tells us about our marriage love, *"Nevertheless let every one of you in particular so love his wife even as himself; and the wife see that she reverence her husband."*

   The meaning of 'reverence' is a feeling or attitude of deep respect, love, and awe, as for something sacred, such as, the vows made together.

5. Should we want the same love from God for our husbands?

   Yes, we can show our love in wanting the same love for him also before God, praying for him, and encouraging him in the Lord. We should not become an obstacle in God's way of accomplishing God's love in him.

6. What does it say about friends in the following verses?

   Proverbs 17:17 *"A friend loveth at all times…"*

   Proverbs 27:6 *"faithful are the wounds of a friend:"*

   Proverbs 27:17 *"Iron sharpenth iron; so a man sharpeneth the countenance of his friend:"*

   Friction causes sparks, and a better countenance should result.

   Song of Solomon 5:16 *"His mouth is most sweet: yea, he is altogether lovely. This is my beloved, and this is my friend, O daughters of Jerusalem."*

   She proclaims he is her husband! Proclaim it! Wear a wedding ring if possible. The Hebrew word for beloved is defined in Strong's Concordance as to boil, to love.

   John 15:13 *"Greater love hath no man than this, that a man lay down his life for his friends."* A well-known saying, we can keep in mind is, "How can we die for Him if we don't live for him?" Speaking of our husbands and them for us, because they are to love us as Christ loved the church and died for it.

7. What actions can we take to show our love for our husbands (and in our next lesson our children)? Listed below are suggestions from godly women as they studied this lesson.

Think about him (them)	Ask him (them) their opinions when making decisions
Pray for him (them)	Maintain identity as a "couple" ("family")
Enjoy his (their) company	Encourage him (them)
Minister to his (their) needs	Go to church together
Respect him as head of the household	Be godly and don't bring him (them) shame, avoid appearance of evil (being evil)
Respect him (them) in front of elders, family, and others	Let him be the leader God expects him to be (this gives him confidence, in finances, tithing, and other areas)

The bible gives guidance for who you should marry and if you should marry, along with other rich marital instructions. Some of those come from The Song of Solomon, Proverbs 31 and 1 Corinthians 7.

Biblical Example of Loving our Husband: Find Priscilla in Acts 18:2,18,26, Romans 16:3, 1 Corinthians 16:19, 2 Timothy 4:19

Priscilla's name is mentioned in the King James Version of the Bible six times, along with her husband Aquila. They are mentioned three times as Aquila and Priscilla and three times as Priscilla and Aquila. Equal in importance. They were Paul's helpers in Christ Jesus, and they all made tents together for their living. Aquila and Priscilla expounded on God's word together, to Apollos. They were a perfect example of a loving couple, having the same goals in love, and spirit. Paul said in Romans 16:3,4, for his life they laid down their own necks. They might have been imprisoned to save Paul for the furtherance of the work of Christ. This might be why Paul asked the people at the church in their home to greet them instead of writing to them himself. Ancient church records show the couple were taken together to an ally way and beheaded for the gospel's sake. This would make them one of the first martyrs of the church. If so, they were loving God and each other, until death. Move over Romeo and Juliet, Aquila and Priscilla loved to an even higher calling.

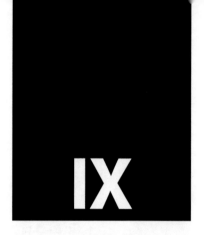

IX

TO LOVE THEIR CHILDREN

Webster's Dictionary says love implies an intense affectionate concern for another, a fondness or deep devotion or a deep and tender feeling for another. In Strong's Concordance the word for love for your children in this passage is *Philoteknos* from the Greek word *philos* which means dear friend and fondness. Strong's also gives indication that the word used as 'love' for your children has ties to the Greek words *timoriq* meaning vindication, a penalty, punishment and *timoreo* to protect one's honor, to avenge, punish.

In the New Testament some men were away preaching and teaching of Christ or being imprisoned or put to death for their beliefs. Which might have left women to do what had been the job of the father. And might be why Strong's Concordance noted the ties to these other Greek words. In Vine's Dictionary *philos* is said to mean tender affection, a friendship, a cherishing above all else except God, and your husband, in the case of children. In another perspective if we love our children and teach them properly, we hopefully can explain why certain things are wrong to do, in a loving way, *"Come now, and let us reason together, saith the LORD: though your sins be as scarlet, they shall be as white as snow; though they be red like crimson, they shall be as wool." Isaiah 1:18*. God is merciful and forgiving, just as we should be to our children. But we should still try to instill right from wrong in our children. We need to guard our honor and our family's honor and discipline or allow our children to be disciplined when necessary, so they may grow up in all things in Christ Jesus. First, and foremost we need to make certain our children know Jesus. We should share with them the reason for the hope that is in us, Jesus.

A. **A Mother's Love, grace in action**

Our children's tender hearts must be established with grace, not meats. See Hebrews 13:9 Keep in mind new Christians hearts also must be established with grace and many Christians often need to be reminded of the grace and forgiveness they have been given.

Hebrews 5:12–14 *"For when for the time ye ought to be teachers, ye have need that one teach you again which be the first principals of the oracles of God; and are become such as have need of milk, and not of strong meat. For every one that useth milk is unskilful in the word of righteousness: for he is a babe. But strong meat belongeth to them that are of full age, even those who by reason of use have their senses exercised to discern both good and evil."*

1. What acts show motherly love?

- Teach children about Jesus and His love for them.
- Teach your children how to pray, acknowledging God and talking to Him.
- Tell children of the hope that is in you because of your belief in Jesus. God's forgiveness of your sins, your new birth into the Family of God, unconditional love from God. Grace which is God's unmerited favor. Mercy from the penalty of sin. Freedom from doing evil. Peace with God and Hope beyond this life.
- Teach them to recognize what is good in others. Like in Proverbs 31:1 *"The words of king Lemuel, the prophecy that his mother taught him."* She taught him about what a good, virtuous wife should be.
- Make sure they are fed. Proverbs 31:15 *"…she giveth meat to her household…"*
- Teach them to study God's word. Deuteronomy 6:6,7 *"And these words, which I command thee this day, shall be in thine heart: And thou shalt teach them diligently unto thy children, and shalt talk of them when thou sittest in thine house, and when thou walkest by the way, and when thou liest down, and when thou risest up."*
- Make sure they are properly clothed. Proverbs 31:21 *"…all her household is clothed with scarlet."*
- Show God's Love, He is Love. Proverbs 31:26 *"She openeth her mouth with wisdom; and in her tongue is the law of kindness."*
- Remember the good things they say and do, especially about God. Like Mary in Luke 2:51 *"but his mother kept all these sayings in her heart."*
- Stand by our children to their death, even humiliating deaths like the cross. John 19:25 *"Now there stood by the cross of Jesus his mother, and his mother's sister, Mary the wife of Cleophas, and Mary Magdalene."*

B. A Mother's Love, a call to Obedience

1. What do the following verses say about instructing our children to be obedient?

- *"…bring them up in the nurture and admonition of the Lord."* Ephesians 6:4
- Help them put on the whole armor of God. Read Ephesians 6:10–18
- Teach them to obey and honor. *"Children, obey your parents in the Lord: for this is right."* Ephesians 6:1
  "Honor thy father and mother; which is the first commandment with promise; That it may be well with thee and thou mayest live long on the earth." Ephesians 6:2,3
- Teach them the two commandments of Jesus, to love God and to love others. *"Thou shalt love the Lord thy God with all thy heart and with all thy soul, and with all thy mind."* Matthew 22:37-40
- Teach them the ten commandments found in Exodus 20, with grace in your heart. No one else will teach them not to lie, cheat, steal, or kill.

2. What do the following verses say about training and discipline as acts of love.

   - Proverbs 22:6 *"Train up a child in the way he should go: and when he is old, he will not depart from it."*
   - Proverbs 13:24 *"He that spareth his rod hateth his son: but he that loveth him chasteneth him betimes."*
   - Proverbs 19:18 *"Chasten thy son while there is hope, and let not thy soul spare for his crying."*
   - Hebrews 12:6,7 *"For whom the Lord loveth he chasteneth, and scourgeth every son whom he receiveth. If ye endure chastening, God dealeth with you as with sons; for what son is he whom the father chasteneth not?"*
   - Hebrews 12:11 *"Now no chastening for the present seemeth to be joyous, but grievous: nevertheless, afterward it yieldeth the peaceable fruit of righteousness unto them which are exercised thereby."*
   - Proverbs 29:15 *"The rod and reproof give wisdom: but a child left to himself bringeth his mother to shame."* In O.T. verses, the Kings were each described as, *"He did that which was right in the eyes of the Lord and his mother was_____."* Or *"He did that which was evil in the eyes of the Lord and his mother was_____."* Read through 1st and 2nd Kings and 2 Chronicles (note 2 Chronicles 25:2) for these Kings and you will learn what they did that was right or evil in the eyes of the Lord. Why is that important to us? Because we mothers are the one who will be in shame.
   - Ephesians 6:4 *"Ye fathers, provoke not your children to wrath: but bring them up in the nurture and admonition of the Lord."* Hopefully fathers will expect their children to honor and respect their mother, it helps make the job mothers have a bit easier. A father gets the glory for well-behaved children. Proverbs 10:1 *"…A wise son maketh a glad father: but a foolish son is the heaviness of his mother."*

3. Who were the Proverbs written to in the above verses?

   Mostly men, Fathers, although the word is meant as an example for us all. *"All scripture is given by God and is profitable for doctrine, for reproof, for correction, and for instruction in righteousness:"* 2Timothy 3:16 Today, both Parents and especially single Christian mothers need to take notice of this.

Biblical Example of Loving Our Children: Find the Elect Lady in 2 John

Although the teaching of the Proverbs 31 woman is good, the New Testament woman has an even higher calling. The elect lady was concerned for her children walking in truth. The truth is that Jesus is the way, the truth, and the life everlasting. But also, she was concerned about how they behaved in that day. This is evident because she had the Apostle John, himself, check on her children. John said he loved her and beseeched her to walk in truth and to love one another and to walk in the commandments. But especially, to love God and love others. John also warned her about deceivers who do not confess that Jesus is God in the flesh, not to wish them well or let them into her house. These children John checked on, must not have been living near their mother as evidenced because John had to write a letter to her. The Elect Lady's children might have been grown. But even if so, she was still concerned about the path they walked in this world and their eternal, spiritual walk with God.

Qualities of Godly (Agape) Love

True Godly love is Charity and Submission. These qualities are so intertwined it is hard to separate them. God loves us this way and gave Himself for us. Showing us that God is love! Love and submission are Christ-like sacrifices. We should show these qualities in ourselves for the benefit of others. These qualities are for our own good and for our husband and children's own good. They bring God glory. *All* Christians are called to this love! If we do not attempt to practice and instruct this true love from God, who will? This love also separates Christians from the world and the lust it lives by. The world does not know this love of God and cannot live by it except in a false attempt. Love comes from Him and was shown by the salvation He provided through His Son. There will come a day when the Holy Spirit leaves this earth, along with God's children. Those left behind will have a harder time finding His love or any love, but He will still make a way for them. They will need to read His word to find out how.

BUILDING RELATIONSHIPS OF LOVE
Qualities of "Godly" Love or Charity is Agape love which is perfect love.
I love you "period." I ♥ U "•"
Webster defines love as an intense, affectionate concern for another.

Love is of God I John 4:7 **"For God so loved the world that He gave his only begotten Son…."** John 3:16
Greater love hath no man than this, that a man lay down his life for his friends. John 15:13
Love God 1 John 5:2   **Love One Another** John 13:34
Women, Love Your Husband Titus 2:4   **Women, Love Your Children** Titus 2:4
Love Your Enemies Matt. 5:44 & Luke 6:27   **God is Love** 1 John 4:16
Husbands Love Your Wives as Christ loved the church Colossians 3:19
But God loved us and while we were yet sinners Christ died for us Romans 5:8

BUILDING RELATIONSHIPS WITH SUBMISSION

Submit to God James 4:7   **Submit to One Another** Ephesians 5:21
Submit to your 'own' Husband Ephesians 5:22   **Children obey your parents** Colossians 3:20
Obey them that have rule over you Hebrews 13:17
Jesus humbled himself becoming obedient unto death, even the death of the cross Philippians 2:8
Strangers shall submit to God: as soon as they hear, they shall be obedient to Him 2 Samuel 22:45

Traits of Godly Submission is submitting to another's Godly Love.
Webster defines submission as: to yield or surrender to the will or authority of another.
We say to surrender to Gods love, and our husbands love is our ultimate love for them.

Discuss how each of the qualities on the next chart would help in the relationship with our husbands and teaching them to our children. The suggestions came from godly woman as they studied this lesson. ***All discussion among us should remain confidential,*** please do not abuse this trust of our sisters in Christ.[2] A blank chart is provided at the end of the book to copy.

---

[2] We might have about eighteen years to teach these things to our children. These precious years go by fast, and we should try to do all we can while they are young to accomplish these teachings. Women have regretted not using those years to mold their children to be Godly and to fulfill God's greater calling.

QUALITIES OF CHARITY 1 CORINTHIANS 13:4–8 ACTS OF SUBMITTING TO ANOTHER'S LOVE	SPOUSE TALKING POINTS	CHILDREN TALKING POINTS
1. **Suffereth Long** (is patient) *"Strengthened with all might, according to his glorious power, unto all patience and longsuffering with joyfulness;" Colossians 1:11* *"Knowing this, that the trying of your faith worketh patience." James 1:3*	God has been patient with us as He molds us. We should slowly react to the trials and behavior of our husbands, and gently guide them to Gods directives.	God has been patient with us as He molds us. Just as we should be patient molding our children by the trials and behaviors they usually, unknowingly, put us through. And gently guide them to Gods directives.
2. **Is Kind** *"And they spake unto him, saying, If thou be kind to this people, and please them, and speak good words to them, they will be thy servants for ever." 2 Chron. 10:7 (see also Psalms 63:3)* *"And be ye kind one to another, tenderhearted, forgiving one another, even as God for Christ's sake hath forgiven you." Ephesians 4:32*	This is a good beginning for a true friendship.	This is a good beginning for a true friendship.
3. **Envieth Not** (not jealous or resentful of another's possessions or qualities) *"Let us walk honestly, as in the day; not in rioting or drunkenness, not in chambering or wantonness, not in strife and envying." Romans 13:13* *"Let us not be desirous of vain glory, provoking one another, envying one another." Galations 5:26*	We should be satisfied so we don't push them for more and more and more.	We should help them be themselves, encourage their qualities and be thankful for them.
4. **Vaunteth not itself** (not boastful) *"Even so the tongue is a little member, and boasteth great things. Behold, how great a matter a little fire kindleth." James 3:5* *"Finally, brethren, whatsoever things are true, whatsoever things are lovely, whatsoever things are honest, whatsoever things are just, whatsoever things are pure, whatsoever things are lovely, Whatsoever things are of good report; if there by any virtue, and if there be any praise, think on these things." Philippians 4:8*	Do not boast about our self or our own accomplishments it can belittle others. We know God had part in it, if not all of it, anyway.	There is always someone better or worse off than them. It is better to try our best than have to be the best or brag about ourselves.

QUALITIES OF CHARITY 1 CORINTHIANS 13:4–8 ACTS OF SUBMITTING TO ANOTHER'S LOVE	SPOUSE TALKING POINTS	CHILDREN TALKING POINTS
5. **Is not puffed up** (not proud, Submission=humility) "Take my yoke upon you, and learn of me; for I am meek and lowly in heart: and ye shall find rest unto your souls." Matthew 11:29 *"Let nothing be done through strife or vainglory; but in lowliness of mind let each esteem other better than themselves" Philippians 2:3*	We all should ask for help when needed, women are the helpmate, but together much can be accomplished.	Encourage them to ask for help and not hold things in, parents, teachers, police, pastors etc. want to help them, not hurt them. Christians should be on watch and hold people in authority to these high standards
6. **Does not behave itself unseemly** (is not rude, avoids the appearance of evil. Submission is to… learn so you never fall) *"Abstain from all appearance of evil. And the very God of peace sanctify you wholly; and I pray God your whole spirit and soul and body be preserved blameless unto the coming of our Lord Jesus Christ." 1 Thessalonians 5:22,23* *"And beside this giving all diligence, add to your faith virtue; and to virtue knowledge; and to knowledge temperance; and to temperance patience; and to patience godliness; and the godliness brotherly kindness; and to brotherly kindness charity. For if these things be in you, and abound, they make you that shall neither be barren nor unfruitful in the knowledge of our Lord Jesus Christ." 2 Peter 1:5–8*	We shouldn't be alone with opposite sex or seek them out over our spouse.	Teach them when they do certain things (like roll their eyes), it seems disrespectful, or that they are trying to be sneaky. Or, when they speak in a certain manner, like with some new slang, it can seem rude. Hanging with a certain crowd might look like they're part of something bad; do they really want to be thought of that way?
7. **Seeketh not her own** (is not self-seeking, not selfish. Submission is to acknowledge His sacrifice) *"I will freely sacrifice unto thee: I will praise thy name, O LORD; for it is good" Psalms 54:6* *"That if thou shalt confess with thy mouth the Lord Jesus, and shalt believe in thine heart that God hath raised him from the dead, thou shalt be saved." Romans 10:9*	Share everything. Work together but acknowledge their sacrifice for us and our family and the family of God.	Share and acknowledge Jesus's sacrifice and mom and dad's sacrifice for them. Honor them and teach that someday they too will have to provide for others.

QUALITIES OF CHARITY 1 CORINTHIANS 13:4–8 ACTS OF SUBMITTING TO ANOTHER'S LOVE	SPOUSE TALKING POINTS	CHILDREN TALKING POINTS
8. Is not easily provoked (not angered or not angered easily like to the point of temper tantrums, even at two or three years old). *"He that is soon angry dealeth foolishly: and a man of wicked devices is hated"* Proverbs 14:17 (see also Matt 5:22) *"A soft answer turneth away wrath: but grievous words stir up anger."* Proverbs 15:1	Learn to reason together with our spouses and our anger should be lessened.	Search out and ask for the reason for things so no one flies off the handle or is soon angry. *"Come now, and let us reason together"* Isaiah 1:18
9. **Thinketh no evil** (keeps no record of wrongs) *"There is therefore now no condemnation to them which are in Christ Jesus, who walk not after the flesh, but after the Spirit."* Romans 8:1 *"Brethren, I count not myself to have apprehended: but this one thing I do, forgetting those things which are behind, and reaching forth unto those things which are before, I press toward the mark for the prize of the high calling of God in Christ Jesus."* Philippians 3:13,14	Forgive and **forget** arguments & trespasses of the past, do not harbor them. Once forgiven, God puts our trespasses as far as east is from west. In other words, He forgives and forgets.	Learn to forgive and **forget** wrongs against them, just as you forgive them. And God forgives us. And they should forgive and forget also. Junior High type indiscretions will come, but these should be learning experiences for us.
10. **Rejoices not in iniquity** (iniquity is sin) *"By this we know that we love the children of God, when we love God, and keep his commandments. For this is the love of God, that we keep his commandments: and his commandments are not grievous."* 1 John 5: 2,3 *"For godly sorrow worketh repentance to salvation not to be repented of: but the sorrow of the world worketh death."* 2 Corinthians 7:10 (see also vs 9)	Better to be sober and mindful of the commandments then to let jesting become rejoicing in iniquity, like laughing at off colored jokes.	Teach that if we are happy at someone else's fall into sin, we do not love in the way God loves us. Do not call other people "fools" or debate God's truths.

QUALITIES OF CHARITY 1 CORINTHIANS 13:4–8 ACTS OF SUBMITTING TO ANOTHER'S LOVE	SPOUSE TALKING POINTS	CHILDREN TALKING POINTS
11. **Rejoices in truth** *"And ye shall know the truth, and the truth shall make you free." John 8:32* *"But speaking the truth in love, may grow up into him in all things, which is the head, even Christ." Eph 4:15* *(See also Ephesians 4: 14–16)*	If our spouse is slipping into sin, point it out in love. Even if they say our breath is bad, be happy they have your best interest at heart and correct it!	When someone (especially you) tells them the truth, they should be happy that someone cares enough to tell them. We have a true friend when they've told us the truth. *"Faithful are the wounds of a friend…"* Proverbs 27:6
12. **Beareth all things** (Beareth is to "put up with" others and the bad things that come to us. Submission is to confess our faults) *"Bear ye one another's burdens, and so fulfil the law of Christ." Galatians 6:2* *"Confess your faults one to another, and pray one for another, that ye may be healed. The effectual fervent prayer of a righteous man availeth much." James 5:16*	Listen to our husbands' problems, their woes, their weaknesses and confess our own faults to them. Then they should not be overcome with too much grief about those things. Pray for forgiveness and healing.	Listen to others needs and confess their own faults to you. This will teach them to realize they too are subject to sin, but they are loved and forgiven when they ask God for forgiveness. Only Jesus was perfect, and he died for their sins. They should pray for others to be saved and healed.
13. **Believeth all things** (submission is to be confident in God and His Word) *"Wherefore also it is contained in scripture, Behold, I lay in Sion a chief corner stone, elect, precious: and he that believeth on him should not be confounded." 1 Pet 2:6 (see also John 3:16)* *"And this is the confidence that we have in him, that, if we ask any thing according to his will, he heareth us." I John 5:14*	Believe your spouse is capable of good things, especially in the Lord. Have confidence that when Gods will and our will are the same, he does answer our prayers.	Your children need to be confident in you as their parent and God as their heavenly father. You and they need to believe that you and they are capable of good things, especially in the Lord.
14. **Hopeth all things** (submission is to seek honor before God in self and others) *"Which hope we have as an anchor of the soul, both sure and stedfast, and which entereth into that within the veil;" Hebrews 6:19* *"To them who by patient continuance in well doing seek for glory and honor and immortality, eternal life." Romans 2:7*	Seek to gain honor before our spouse and hope to present each other to God without spot or blemish. Hope in God to accomplish great things in them and us.	Seek to attain honor in all that they do for their parents and God and hope for that blessed assurance. Hope in God is the anchor of the soul. Even if parents are not honorable people themselves, the children should seek to be honorable.

QUALITIES OF CHARITY 1 CORINTHIANS 13:4–8 *ACTS OF SUBMITTING TO ANOTHER'S LOVE*	SPOUSE TALKING POINTS	CHILDREN TALKING POINTS
15. **Endureth all things** (submission is to endure chastening) *"Praise ye the Lord. O give thanks unto the Lord; for he is good: for his mercy endureth for ever." Psalms 106:1* *"If ye endure chastening, God dealeth with you as with sons; for what son is he whom the father chasteneth not?" Hebrews 12:7*	Even if your spouse's chastisement seems unfair or too critical, endure until the end and thereby grow and fulfill the will of the Lord. (Reason together)	If chastisement seems unfair or too critical, they need to endure until the end. Its purpose is so they will grow up to know right from wrong. It still is okay to reason together.
16. **Never fails** (submission is to trust in Him) *"Heaven and earth shall pass away, but my words shall not pass away." Matthew 24:35* *"Though he slay me, yet will I trust in him:…." Job 13:15*	Reassure our spouse that we will be by their side through thick and thin, to the end. Just as Jesus is with us.	Even if all the world and all the people in it fail them, God will not fail them. Jesus died to save them! He will always have their backs and hopefully you will too, to the end!

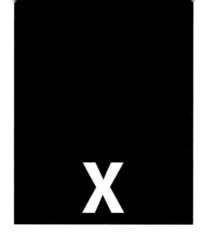

TO BE DISCREET

Webster defines being discreet as: Having a judicious reserve in speech or behavior, unpretentious. Being discreet has been defined as, saying, and doing the right thing, in the right way, at the right time. Others define being discreet as; the ability to avoid words, actions and attitudes that could result in undesirable consequences. In Vine's and Strong's, the word "discreet" comes from the Greek word, *sophron*, its meaning is: Sound mind, self-controlled, sane, temperate, sensible.

So, to be discreet goes even deeper than our actions and attitudes. Being discreet helps us to think soundly and protect our minds from irrational and unsound thinking. This thinking gives us the ability to be careful about what one says or does; the ability to keep silent or to speak up, to act or to refrain from acting. Being discreet preserves confidences when needed. Biblically, to be discreet, like discretion, is a judicial understanding of God's will or judging and understanding what is right and what is wrong. Think on God's word; do all to understand it and judge it to be right. *Being Discreet is to be intelligent; to think, judge and understand.*

A. Being discreet has to do with understanding. Understanding makes the knowledge we have of God, sensible. It makes sense to us and makes us want to hide it in our heart. It is not just memory work. Pray for knowledge and understanding. Being discreet is understanding.

1. From Philippians 4:6,7 show what benefits you will obtain if you

    "Be careful for nothing; but in every thing by prayer and supplication with thanksgiving let your requests be made known unto God. And the peace of God, which passeth all understanding, shall keep your hearts and minds through Christ Jesus."

2. In Phil 2:2 Paul states

    "Fulfil ye my joy, that ye be likeminded, having the same love, being of one accord, of one mind:"

    How can this protect us? Having these same attributes means other temptations, lifestyles, and choices the world makes won't affect us as much in the church body. If one brother or sister falls others could be tempted and fall also. Our world has been steadily slipping away from His truth and it shows in our families, our jobs, and our governments, our nations and sadly even in some of our churches.

This study is not about any one person. It is about GOD and His plan for His women. Remember God's forgiveness, truth, and grace is in His Son!

3. This ministry is meant to help God's women understand His will and why He wants us to be discreet, among other things. What did the Eunuch tell Philip in Acts 8:31?

Philip asked the eunuch if he understood the scripture he was reading *"And he said, How can I, except some man should guide me? And he desired Philip that he would come up and sit with him."* We should guide our women, especially our young women fulfilling this principal, to help them understand.

B. To be discreet; has to do with the way we feel, judge, and determine. It comprises the faculties of perception and trust. When we perceive the truth, we will know it! We will understand it, we will trust it, we will feel it, we will love it. We can make our judgments and determinations from it. Pray for wisdom to use our knowledge and understanding in the Lord. Being discreet is wise!

1. From Proverbs 3:13&21 show that discretion and understanding are similar in their effect. What other good qualities are mentioned in these verses?

Happiness. *"Happy is the man that findeth wisdom, and the man that getteth understanding."* Proverbs 3:13

"My son, let not them depart from thine eyes: keep sound wisdom and discretion:" Proverbs 3:21

God's sound wisdom in His word and the discretion or understanding we obtain from it makes us happy! We should trust God's wisdom. One day we will also be happy to be used by God because of this teaching.

2. Knowledge is what we learn, knowledge, wisdom and discretion is what we put on our heart. How do these qualities of discretion benefit us? See Proverbs 3:22–24

"So shall they be life unto thy soul, and grace to thy neck. Then shalt thou walk in thy way safely, and thy foot shall not stumble. When thou liest down, thou shalt not be afraid: yea, thou shalt lie down, and thy sleep shall be sweet." Grace to the neck helps you hold your head high.

3. Since I am being taught in church and by the women of the church, how can I become a discreet woman myself? See Proverbs 5:1,2

"My son, attend unto my wisdom and bow thine ear to my understanding: That thou mayest regard discretion, and that thy lips may keep knowledge." Make discretion a priority. Use it, love it and its practical, sound wisdom for us.

4. Will I have regrets if I do not practice being discreet?

See Proverbs 9-15 for benefits of discretion and regrets of not having discretion. Highlight these verses in two distinct colors: one for the benefits of wisdom and discretion and one color for the regrets of not having wisdom and discretion. Teachers may see the highlighted pages of Proverbs at the end of this lesson. To help women remember this lesson provide two different colored highlighters for each of the women you are teaching. You can mark your Bibles together, highlighting the benefits first and then highlighting the regrets.

5. What is the biblical opinion (God's opinion) of a woman without discretion? See Proverbs 11:22

"As a jewel of gold in a swine's snout, so is a fair woman which is without discretion."

A fair woman without discretion is thought of by God as a jewel of gold, even though it is in a swine's snout, instead of being in the very loving arms of God. This should remind us that we women are precious in the sight of God. In some religions, even some Christian religions, the Bible is not taught. And even though they have a 'saving' faith, they think being discreet is just man's opinion against the world and not the very calling of God. Through this study and with the prayers of other women, we can all realize this calling.

C. Demonstrations or acts of being discreet. We may be the weaker vessels, which might mean we are physically, emotionally, and spiritually weaker. Regardless, we are not helpless if we are in Christ. God will help us, especially if we ask Him. And we can gain strength with each other.

1. What does Proverbs 17:27–28 tell us about being sparing of words in our speech?

"He that hath knowledge spareth his words: and a man of understanding is of an excellent spirit. Even a fool, when he holdeth his peace, is counted wise: and he that shutteth his lips is esteemed a man of understanding."

2. Proverbs 19:11 tells us of something discretion can do for us, what is it?

"The discretion of a man deferreth his anger; and it is his glory to pass over a transgression." So, indiscretion is the direct opposite in a person and is quick to anger and might never forgive the wrong doer.

3. Proverbs 19:8 tells us more, what?

"He that getteth wisdom loveth his own soul: he that keepeth understanding shall find good." Ask for wisdom and understanding and we will find good.

4. It might be easier to be discreet if we are prone to a meek and quiet spirit. We can all be led by the Spirit of God, allowing Him to remind us of what we know from God's word. What is a meek and quiet spirit?

Meek, according to Strong's Concordance is to be humble and mild. A quiet spirit is to be of a quiet mental disposition or quiet mind, our mouth should follow. This is strength under control. What does Matthew 11:29 say? *"Take my yoke upon you and learn of me; for I am meek and lowly in heart: and ye shall find rest unto your souls."* Hear that still, small, voice of God. Praise God for His spirit.

5. How do we perceive God's word?

Some people think this is ancient stuff and it does not work for today's modern world. Proverbs Chapters 9–14 should be reread by them if they still think this. Wisdom is ageless and comes from God's Holy word! It encourages us, exhorts us, and corrects us, even today! Christians have found these things to be true, either by living by them or from the experience of not living by them and needing to repent. Again, together, we Christian women need each other for the world we have to face. And this might be even more evident as time goes on.

6. Can we determine right from wrong from God's word?

Yes.

7. Can you trust God's word?

The word of God shows us how to be saved and how to live a good life before God. It is for us and the whole family of God. We need to ask the Holy Spirit for wisdom and understanding, discretion, so it will make sense to us. Ask any Christian woman or pastor or teacher for help in learning how to be discreet. They should not want anyone to fall from a lack of understanding God's truths.

8. Why tell me what to think or how to think?

God's word tells us in Philippians 4:8 *"Finally, brethren, whatsoever things are true, whatsoever things are honest, whatsoever things are just, whatsoever things are pure, whatsoever things are lovely, whatsoever things are of good report; if there be any virtue and if there be any praise, think on these things."*

In this study we see God is good and His word is good. The purpose of this lesson is to accomplish in us self-respect and respect for others. And all the good benefits from being discreet; the knowledge, wisdom, understanding, and happiness that it provides. The benefits of being discreet is for ourselves, our family, and all those around us, not to harm us.

D. Summary

We do not have to believe everything others *say*, like, "How could God love you when He gave you such a terrible life?" or "look at all the things you have had to deal with, whatever they are…divorce, illness, death, etc.". or "God couldn't love you or me that is just for people with good lives." We do not have to *do* everything others do, either. We can be the vessels for truth by being discreet. His word points to the fact that He does love us all and wants us to have a good life and future with Him. Pray that He puts other Christians around us that care for us to our very souls. If we know other Christians who are struggling, try to seek them out and lead them in God's specific teachings or find someone who will. *"I will call upon the LORD, who is worthy to be praised: so shall I be saved from my enemies."* Psalms 18:3

God loves us, just like He loved Sarah and shut up the wombs of the entire nation of Egypt to protect her. Like Rahab in Joshua 2–6 who with the wisdom of her heart hid the spies. Knowing the God of Israel was the true God. Like Esther and her bravery to go before the king and risk her life. Like Ruth, with her devotion to her mother-in-law, Naomi. And like Mary in the New Testament who was blessed among women and bore the Christ child, Jesus. He loves His women. He loves all the New Testament women like us, who have chosen to believe on Him! This world cannot hope for more for us than He hopes for us. If we doubt His love because our life has become hard, please remember the sacrifice He made by giving His own life on the cross for us. Choose to be discreet, do all to understand. Judge that His word is right, be wise and see ourselves as God sees us, through the lens of His Son.

An example of these lessons was once heard on Christian radio. A panel was talking about knowing the difference of knowledge, wisdom, discretion, prudence, and soberness. They illustrated, that we know that a tomato is a fruit because it grows on the vine, that is *knowledge*. However, we would not want a tomato in a fruit salad, which is *wisdom*. When we thought about it, we judged that the tomato would not taste good in the salad . That 'thinking on' whether to put tomatoes in a fruit salad was using our knowledge, wisdom, understanding, and judgement, that is *discretion*. Then, we will plan to put other fruit in the salad, which is *prudence*. And we would make and bring the fruit salad without the tomatoes to a church gathering. That is *soberness*, or action.

E. Application

With discretion we can make rational decisions about how we live our lives before God and be strong in those decisions. With prudence/planning and soberness/action we can live a life that is not out of control.

1. **'Knowledge'** is having knowledge of God and the wisdom of his word, putting it in our mind and on our heart. *"The fear of the Lord is the beginning of wisdom: and the knowledge of the holy is understanding."* Proverbs 9:10 (Think and Know)

2. Being **'Discreet'** or using **'Discretion'** understands and judges the wisdom of what God has told us. That it is good. Understanding will protect our mind and heart from wandering into unknown territories. 'Think on' His word, and 'understand it' which is wise. *"Wherefore be ye not unwise, but understanding what the will of the Lord is."* Ephesians 5:17 (Think, Judge and Understand)

3. **'Prudence'** Proverbs 14:15 tells us to be prudent: *"The simple believeth every word: but the prudent man looketh well to his going."* Webster's Dictionary says prudence is managing carefully and with economy. Prudence is also said to be planning. This is needed because many people believe and do everything other people, who do not have their best interest at heart, tell them. Instead of doing what God tells them. They want to lead them to fit in with the world or to their way of thinking. We need to plan for what we should do in certain situations by God's standards. (Think and Plan)

4. **'Soberness'** is putting in practice the bodily action of self-control. Which results from the practice of the above traits. Listening to the inner voice and choose to do or act out what would most glorify God and for yourself. (Think and Act) See the lesson "To Be Sober".

On the next page, situations are listed that could happen in our lives and as we study God's word it shows us how to use wisdom, discretion, prudence, and soberness to deal with them. Discussion and support among other Christian women can help us with this lesson. The more situations where we know God's will; the more we can try to understand His reasoning. The more we plan for situations the more likely we will act, to please God. We will not have to take time thinking about it, if, or when it occurs because you already set your mind and made your plan of action. The following situations are examples and not meant to be dictates. Please continue conversations, they can be greatly beneficial, especially for younger women. A blank form is provided at end of book for you to copy.

Biblical Example of being Discreet: Find Mary of Bethany in Mark 6, 15 and 16, Luke 10, John 11 and possibly as one of the other Mary's mentioned in the New Testament.

Mary was the sister of Martha and Lazarus. She listened to Jesus' word as she sat at His feet soaking His word into her Spirit and applying it to her life. Jesus loved Mary and her family, and it is evident she loved Him. We all should be in prayer for God's strength, forgiveness, and grace in our lives. If, somehow, we fail to meet up to Mary's reputation for listening to Jesus.

SITUATIONS	KNOWLEDGE	DISCRETION Understanding, Judgement & Wisdom	PRUDENCE Planning	SOBERNESS Self-control/ Action
I am asked to steal	God says, "Thou shalt not steal"	I understand God wants to take care of me and I judge that God will supply all my needs. He wants me to have faith in Him for things I need. Stealing could hurt the person (or company) it belongs to. They must need it more than me or God would have already given it to me. Stealing undermines our society and eventually costs us all. I should not even steal a persons' reputation from them by talking badly of them to others.	My plan is to not let the **lust of my eyes** control me. If I am asked to steal, I will say, "NO!" and tell the person who wanted me to steal why it is wrong before God and man. I will suggest that we could work together to buy it. I will walk away and not think or talk about it. I will return borrowed things so I will not be thought of as a thief. I will walk away or at least change the subject if gossip starts.	I will act by not stealing and by telling this person who must not know or understand that stealing is wrong that it is against God and my better judgment. I will not steal, not even a person's reputation. Stealing is an unlawful act. I will not have contact with this person if they do not stop. I will pray for them. If, they are sorry & stop I will be a friend and ask them to church.
I am asked to drink alcohol or take drugs	God says not to become drunken. He also says to avoid the appearance of evil.	I understand God has my best interest at heart. I have judged that He loves me and wants the best for my life. I now have the wisdom to know, if I do these things, it could ruin my relationships with my family, affect my mind and thinking and bring me physical or mental harm. It could make me do things I would not normally do. I would have regrets and a bad testimony before God and man.	My plan is to not live in the **pride of life**, thinking that I need to please myself and others. If I am asked to do these things, I will not! I plan to leave the party or person's home. I plan to get away or call my parents or husband and ask them to pick me up. I will not give them time to try to convince me. I will avoid situations that would cause me to be tempted in this way.	I will act by getting away from this temptation. I will avoid people trying to press me to do things that can cause themselves or me harm. I will explain to them how it can harm them, especially if they profess to be Christians to help protect one of God's own. If, they are sorry I will be a friend. Pray for them and ask them to church.

| I am tempted to have sex with someone other than my husband | God says not to commit adultery or fornication | Sexual disease is rampant in this world. I understand God wants to protect my body from these. I have judged that I, my spouse, and family or future family could suffer from this, physically and emotionally. I have wisdom to know that as God's child; my life would be full of regrets, and I could no longer trust myself or others. It would also be a hindrance to my walk with God. | My plan is to be chaste and not carnal. I will marry first before having sex. To be carnal is the fulfilling of the *lust of the flesh*. The Bible says to "flee fornication" and that is my plan. I also will not be alone with a member of the other sex (or same sex if I think they are gay) so as to avoid "the appearance of evil". | I will act by doing all I can to be observant of any situation that could become tempting or threatening. I will run from the situation. I will not care if anyone laughs at me or says I am crazy. I will do all to keep my plan of action. I will pray for them. |

Pink Highlights: Benefits of Wisdom   Green Highlights: Regrets of not having Wisdom

Proverbs 9

1. Wisdom hath builded her house, she had hewn out of her seven pillars:
2. She hath killed her beasts; She hath mingled her wine; She has also furnished her table.
3. She hath set forth her maidens: she crieth upon the highest places of the city,
4. Whoso is simple, let him turn in hither: as for him that wanteth understanding, she saith to him,
5. Come, eat of my bread, and drink of the wine which I have mingled.
6. Forsake the foolish, and live; and go in the way of understanding.
7. He that reproveth a scorner getteth himself shame: and he that rebuketh a wicked man getteth himself a blot.
8. Reprove not a scorner, lest he hate thee: rebuke a wise man, and he will love thee.
9. Give instruction to a wise man, and he will be yet wiser: teach a just man, and he will increase in learning.
10. The fear of the LORD is the beginning of wisdom: and the knowledge of the holy is understanding.
11. For by me thy days shall be multiplied, and the years of their life shall be increased.
12. If thou be wise, thou shalt be wise for thyself: but if thou scornest, thou alone shalt bear it.
13. A foolish woman is clamorous: she is simple, and knoweth nothing.
14. For she sitteth at the door of her house, on a seat in the high places of the city,
15. To call passengers who go right on their ways:
16. Whoso is simple, let him turn in hither: and as for him that wanteth understanding, she saith to him,
17. Stolen waters are sweet, and bread eaten in secret is pleasant.
18. But he knoweth not that the dead are there; and that her guests are in the depths of hell.

Proverbs 10

1. The proverbs of Solomon. A wise son maketh a glad father: but a foolish son is the heaviness of his mother.
2. Treasures of wickedness profit nothing: but righteousness delivereth from death.
3. The Lord will not suffer the soul of the righteous to famish: but he casteth away the substance of the wicked.
4. He becometh poor that dealeth with a slack hand: but the hand of the diligent maketh rich.
5. He that gathereth in the summer is a wise son: but he that sleepeth in the harvest is a son that causes shame.
6. Blessings are upon the head of the just: but violence covereth the mouth of the wicked.
7. The memory of the just is blessed: but the name of the wicked shall rot.
8. The wise in heart will receive commandments: but a prating fool shall fall.
9. He that walketh uprightly walketh surely: but he that perverteth his ways shall be known.
10. He that winketh with the eye causes sorrow: but a prating fool shall fall.
11. The mouth of a righteous man is a well of life: but violence covereth the mouth of the wicked.
12. Hatred stirreth up strifes: but love covereth all sins.
13. In the lips of him that hath understanding wisdom is found: but a rod is for the back of him that his void of understanding.
14. Wise men lay up knowledge: but the mouth of the foolish is near destruction.
15. The rich man's wealth is his strong city: the destruction of the poor is their poverty.

16. The labor of the righteous tendeth to life: the fruit of the wicked to sin.
17. He is in the way of life that keepeth instruction: that he that refuseth reproof erreth.
18. He that hideth hatred with lying lips, and he that uttereth a slander, is a fool.
19. In the multitude of words there wanteth not sin: but he that refrain his lips is wise.
20. The tongue of the just is as choice silver: the heart of the wicked is little worth.
21. The lips of the righteous feed many: but fools die for want of wisdom.
22. The blessing of the LORD, it maketh rich, and he addeth no sorrow with it.
23. It is as sport to a fool to do mischief: but a man of understanding hath wisdom.
24. The fear of the wicked, it shall come upon him: but the desire of the righteous shall be granted.
25. As a whirlwind passeth, so is the wicked man no more: but the righteous is an everlasting foundation.
26. As vinegar to the teeth, and as smoke to the eyes, so is the sluggard to them that send him.
27. The fear of the LORD prolongeth days: but the years of the wicked shall be shortened.
28. The hope of the righteous shall be gladness: but the expectation of the wicked shall perish.
29. The way of the Lord is strength to the upright: but destruction shall be to the workers of iniquity.
30. The righteous shall never be removed: but the wicked shall not inhabit the earth.
31. The mouth of the just bringeth forth wisdom: but the froword tongue shall be cut out.
32. The lips of the righteous know what is acceptable: but the mouth of the wicked speaketh frowordness.

Proverbs 11

1. A false balance is an abomination to the LORD: but a just weight is his delight.
2. When pride cometh, then cometh shame: but with the lowly is wisdom.
3. The integrity of the upright shall guide them: but the perverseness of transgressors shall destroy them.
4. Riches profit not in the day of wrath: but righteousness delivereth from death.
5. The righteousness of the perfect shall direct his way: but the wicked shall fall by his own wickedness.
6. The righteousness of the upright shall deliver them: but transgressors shall be taken in their own naughtiness.
7. When a wicked man dieth his expectation shall perish: and the hope of unjust men perisheth.
8. The righteous is delivered out of trouble, and the wicked cometh in his stead.
9. An hypocrite with his mouth destroyeth his neighbor: but through knowledge shall the just be delivered.
10. When it goeth well with the righteous, the city rejoiceth: and when the wicked perish, there is shouting.
11. By the blessing of the upright the city is exalted: but it is overthrown by the mouth of the wicked.
12. He that is void of wisdom despiseth his neighbor: but a man of understanding holdeth his peace.
13. A talebearer revealeth secrets: but he that is of a faithful spirit concealeth the matter.
14. Where no counsel is, the people fall: but in the multitude of counsellers there is safety.
15. He that is surety for a stranger shall smart for it: and he hateth suretiship is sure.
16. A gracious woman retaineth honour: and strong men retain riches.
17. The merciful man doeth good to his own soul: but he that is cruel troubleth his own flesh.
18. The wicked worketh a deceitful work: but to him that soweth righteousness shall be a sure reward.
19. As righteousness tendeth to life: so he that pursueth evil pursueth it to his own death.
20. They that are of a froword heart are abomination to the LORD: but such as are upright in their way are his delight.
21. Though hand join in hand, the wicked shall not be unpunished: but the seed of the righteous shall be delivered.

22. As a jewel of gold in a swine's snout, so is a fair woman which is without discretion.
23. The desire of the righteous is only good: but the expectation of the wicked is wrath.
24. There is that scattereth, and yet increaseth; and there is that withholdeth more than is meet, but it tendeth to poverty.
25. The liberal soul shall be made fat: and he that watereth shall be watered also himself.
26. He that withholdeth corn, the people shall curse him: but blessing shall be upon the head of him that selleth it.
27. He that diligently seeketh good procureth favour: but he that seeketh mischief, it shall come unto him.
28. He that trusteth in his riches shall fall: but the righteous shall flourish as a branch.
29. He that troubleth his own house shall inherit the wind: and the fool shall be servant to the wise of heart.
30. The fruit of the righteous is a tree of life; and he that winneth souls is wise.
31. Behold, the righteous shall be recompensed in the earth: much more the wicked and the sinner.

Proverbs 12

1. Whoso loveth instruction loveth knowledge: but he that hateth reproof is brutish.
2. A good man obtaineth favour of the LORD: but a man of wicked devices will he condemn.
3. A man shall not be established by wickedness: but the root of the righteous shall not be moved.
4. A virtuous woman is a crown to her husband: but she that make it ashamed is as rottenness in his bones.
5. The thoughts of the righteous are right: but the counsels of the wicked are deceit.
6. The words of the wicked are to lie in wait for blood: but the mouth of the upright shall deliver them.
7. The wicked are overthrown, and are not: but the house of the righteous shall stand.
8. A man shall be commended according to his wisdom: but he that is of a perverse heart shall be despised.
9. He that is despised and hath a servant: is better than he that honoureth himself, and lack of bread.
10. A righteous man regardeth the life of his beast: but the tender mercies of the wicked are cruel.
11. He that tilleth his land shall be satisfied with bread: that he that followeth with vain persons is void of understanding.
12. The wicked desireth the net of evil men: but the root of the righteous yieldeth fruit.
13. The wicked is snared by the transgression of his lips: but the just shall come out of trouble.
14. A man shall be satisfied with good by the fruit of his mouth: and the recompense of a man's hands shall be rendered unto him.
15. The way of a fool is right in his own eyes: but he that harkeneth unto counsel is wise.
16. A fool's wrath is presently known: but a prudent man covereth shame.
17. He that speaketh truth sheweth forth righteousness: but a false witness deceit.
18. There is that speaketh like the piercings of a sword: but the tongue of the wise is health.
19. The lip of truth shall be established for ever: but a lying tongue is but for a moment.
20. Deceit is in the heart of them that imagine evil: but to the counsellers of peace is joy.
21. There shall no evil happen to the just: but the wicked shall be filled with mischief.
22. Lying lips are abomination to the LORD: but they that deal truly are his delight.
23. A prudent man concealeth knowledge: but the heart of fools proclaimeth foolishness.
24. The hand of the diligent shall bear rule: but the slothful shall be under tribute.
25. Heaviness in the heart of man maketh it stoop: but a good word maketh it glad.
26. The righteous is more excellent than his neighbor: but the way of the wicked seduceth them.

27. The slothful man roasteth not that which he took in hunting: but the substance of a diligent man is precious.
28. In the way of righteousness is life; and in the pathway thereof there is no death.

Proverbs 13

1. A wise son heareth his father's instruction: but a scorner heareth not rebuke.
2. A man shall eat good by the fruit of his mouth: but the soul of the transgressors shall eat violence.
3. He that keepeth his mouth keepeth his life: but he that openeth wide his lips shall have destruction.
4. The soul of the sluggard desireth, and hath nothing: but the soul of the diligent shall be made fat.
5. A righteous man hateth lying: but a wicked man is loathsome, and cometh to shame.
6. Righteousness keepeth him that is upright in the way: but wickedness overthroweth the sinner.
7. There is that maketh himself rich, yet hath nothing: there is that maketh himself poor, yet hath great riches.
8. The ransom of a man's life are his riches: but the poor heareth not rebuke.
9. The light of the righteous rejoiceth: but the lamp of the wicked shall be put out.
10. Only by pride cometh contention: but with the well advised is wisdom.
11. Wealth gotten by vanity shall be diminished: but he that gathereth by labour shall increase.
12. Hope deferred make it the heart sick: but when the desire cometh, it is a tree of life.
13. Whoso despiseth the word shall be destroyed: but he that feareth the commandment shall be rewarded.
14. The law of the wise is a fountain of life, to depart from the snares of death.
15. Good understanding giveth favour: but the way transgressors is hard.
16. Every prudent man dealeth with knowledge: but a fool layeth open his folly.
17. A wicked messenger falleth into mischief: but a faithful ambassador is health.
18. Poverty and shame shall be to him that refuseth instruction: but he that regardeth reproof shall be honoured.
19. The desire accomplished is sweet to the soul: but it is abomination to fools to depart from evil.
20. He that walketh with wise men shall be wise: but a companion of fools shall be destroyed.
21. Evil pursueth sinners: but to the righteous good shall be repaid.
22. A good man leaveth an inheritance to his children's children: and the wealth of the sinner is laid up for the just.
23. Much food is in the tillage of the poor: but there is that is destroyed for want of judgment.
24. He that spareth his rod hateth his son: but he that loveth him chaseneth him betimes.
25. The righteous eateth to the satisfying of his soul: but the belly of the wicked shall want.

Proverbs 14

1. Every wise woman buildeth her house: but the foolish plucketh it down with her hands.
2. He that walketh in his uprightness feareth the LORD: but he that is perverse in his ways despiseth him.
3. In the mouth of the foolish is a rod of pride: but the lips of the wise shall preserve them.
4. Where no oxen are, the crib is clean: but much increase is by the strength of the ox.
5. A faithful witness will not lie: but a false witness will utter lies.
6. A scorner seeketh wisdom, and findeth it not: but knowledge is easy unto him that understandeth.
7. Go from the presence of a foolish man, when thou perceivest not in him the lips of knowledge.
8. The wisdom of the prudent is to understand his way: but the folly of fools is deceit.

9. Fools make a mock at sin: but among the righteous there is favour.
10. The heart knoweth his own bitterness; and a stranger does not intermeddle with his joy.
11. The house of the wicked shall be overthrown: but the tabernacle of the upright shall flourish.
12. There is a way which seemeth right unto a man, but the end thereof are the ways of death.
13. Even in laughter the heart is sorrowful; and the end of that mirth is heaviness.
14. The backslider in heart shall be filled with his own ways: and a good man shall be satisfied from himself.
15. The simple believeth every word: but the prudent man looketh well to his going.
16. A wise man feareth, and departeth from evil: but the fool rageth and is confident.
17. He that is soon angry dealeth foolishly: And a man of wicked devices is hated.
18. The simple inherit folly: but the prudent are crowned with knowledge.
19. The evil bow before the good; and the wicked at the gates of the righteous.
20. The poor is hated even of his own neighbor: but the rich hath many friends.
21. He that despiseth his neighbor sinneth: but he that hath mercy on the poor: happy is he.
22. Do they not err that devise evil? But mercy and truth shall be to them that devise good.
23. In all labour there is profit: but the talk of the lips tendeth only to penury.
24. The crown of the wise is the riches: but the foolishness of fools is folly.
25. A true witness delivereth souls: but a deceitful witness speaketh lies.
26. In the fear of the LORD is strong confidence: and his children shall have a place of refuge.
27. The fear of the LORD is a fountain of life, to depart from the snares of death.
28. In the multitude of people is the kings honour: but in the want of people is destruction of the prince.
29. He that is slow to wrath is of great understanding: but he that is hasty of spirit exalteth folly.
30. A sound heart is a life of the flesh: but envy the rottenness of the bones.
31. He that oppresseth the poor reproacheth his Maker: but he that honoureth him hath mercy on the poor.
32. The wicked is driven away in his wickedness: but the righteous hath hope in his death.
33. Wisdom resteth in the heart of him that hath understanding: but that which is in the midst of fools is made known.
34. Righteousness exalteth a nation: but sin is a reproach to any people.
35. The King's favor is toward a wise servant: but his wrath is against him that causeth shame.

Proverbs 15

1. A soft answer turneth away wrath: but grievous words stir up anger.
2. The tongue of the wise useth knowledge aright: but the mouth of fools poureth out foolishness.
3. The eyes of the Lord are in every place, beholding the evil and the good.
4. A wholesome tongue is a tree of life: but perverseness therein is a breach in the spirit.
5. A fool despiseth his father's instruction: but he that regardeth reproof is prudent.
6. In the house of the righteous is much treasure: but in the revenues of the wicked is trouble.
7. The lips of the wise disperse knowledge: but the heart of the foolish doeth not so.
8. The sacrifice of the wicked is an abomination to the LORD: but the prayer of the upright is his delight.
9. The way of the wicked is an abomination unto the LORD: but he loveth them that followeth after righteousness.
10. Correction is grievous unto him that forsaketh the way: and he that hateth reproof shall die.
11. Hell and destruction are before the LORD: how much more then the hearts of the children of men?
12. A scorner loveth not one that reproveth him: neither will he go unto the wise.

13. A merry heart maketh a cheerful countenance: but by sorrow of the heart the spirit is broken.
14. The heart of him that hath understanding seeketh knowledge: but the mouth of fools feedeth on foolishness.
15. All the days of the afflicted are evil: but he that is of a merry heart hath a continual feast.
16. Better is little with the fear of the LORD than great treasure with trouble therewith.
17. Better is a dinner of herbs where love is, than a stalled ox and hatred therewith.
18. A wrathful man stirreth up strife: but he that is slow to anger appeaseth strife.
19. The way of the slothful man is an hedge of thorns: but the way of the righteous is made plain.
20. A wise son maketh a glad father: but a foolish man despiseth his mother.
21. Folly is joy to him that is destitute of wisdom: but a man of understanding walketh uprightly.
22. Without counsel purposes are disappointed: but in the multitude of counsellers they are established.
23. A man hath joy by the answer of his mouth: and a word spoken in due season, how good is it!
24. The way of life is above to the wise, that he may depart from hell beneath.
25. The Lord will destroy the house of the proud: but he will establish the border of the widow.
26. The thoughts of the wicked are an abomination to the LORD: but the words of the pure are pleasant words.
27. He that is greedy of gain troubleth his own house; but he that hateth gifts shall live.
28. The heart of the righteous studieth to answer: but the mouth of the wicked poureth out evil things.
29. The Lord is far from the wicked: but he heareth the prayer of the righteous.
30. The light of the eyes rejoiceth the heart: and a good report make the bones fat.
31. The ear that heareth the reproof of life abideth among the wise.
32. He that refuseth instruction despiseth his own soul: but he that heareth reproof getteth understanding.
33. The fear of the LORD is the instruction of wisdom; and before honour is humility.

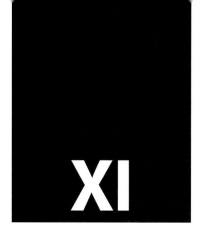

XI

CHASTE

The Strong's Concordance uses the Greek word *hagnos* for chaste; to be clean, innocent, modest, pure. Vine's Dictionary says it means pure from carnality. These are the Christian traits for being chaste and they apply to our heart, our conscience (thoughts) and our bodies. Being chaste as a Christian is ridiculed by the world. But in fact, Christianity, and some other religions; are the only places in our world that it is cherished and encouraged. Being chaste provides a safe haven for a happy soul, spirit and body, a good life.

As the body and bride of Christ we are called to be chaste. The problem is that our fast paced, self-gratifying world doesn't want to allow room *for the freedom of our choice* to be chaste or free from carnality. It is due to our freedom or liberty in Christ that we can stand against the world system. Liberty means, we are freed from the bonds of sin and the flesh. All have sinned. We should avoid sin and are freed from the bonds of it. God can break our chains of bondage with the help of the Holy Spirit. We do not have to be enslaved to sin or the flesh. We should rejoice and hold on to this liberty.

This portion of our study emphasizes the fact that it is our right to keep our body pure and our church pure from the world and Jesus will give us the strength to accomplish it. He gives us a way to escape the corruption of the world. As we grow in knowledge, grace, and the love of God, becoming more spiritual; it is much easier to be chaste and escape that corruption. This shows the need of *aged* women teaching our *younger* women. To help them be strong in their walk with the Lord. We can overcome carnality because we learn that; there is only a 'good intention' from God for us. At times, these things are what our own nature wars against. By being chaste we can avoid heartache and hurting others. We should pray and ask for God's strength to overcome our own sinful nature and the effects of the world. We might be the weaker vessel but, *"I can do all things through Christ which strengtheneth me."* Philippians 4:13

This study is not about any one person. It is about GOD and His plan for His women. Remember God's forgiveness, truth, and grace is in His Son!

A. To be chaste is to be pure from carnality or to not be governed by human nature.

We all have a carnal nature; it is human nature. We all need to know, understand, plan for, and act, to be pure before God and allow Him to fulfill all our needs. It is good to remember that the power to be chaste comes from God so that we are not "*Having a form of godliness, but denying the power thereof:*" 2 Timothy 3:5 If we boast about being chaste, we are not giving God the credit due Him for His strengthening our resolve to be chaste. Also, carnality leads to more and more sin in a person's life, which is against God. A Christian must trust and have faith that God's power can and will work to give us a way to escape carnality. So, be aware of ways to escape, such as marriage or abstinence to escape fornication. Being chaste in our physical walk with God is mostly what we will address in this lesson. However, being chaste is also a mental battle. Allowing or dwelling on wrong thoughts about God such as Him not loving us, can affect our spiritual walk also. By having faith and drenching ourselves in God's word we will not believe the lies of Satan as told through other people. Things we are to avoid are fornication which is sex outside of marriage. And adultery, which is sexual sin between a married person and someone other than their spouse.

Sanctification is being set apart from the world. Being modest in dress can set us apart from the world. The things listed above can help preserve our chasteness and help us avoid sexual sin.

1. What does 1Thessalonians 4:3,4 say about our bodies?

   "*This is the will of God, even your sanctification, that ye should abstain from fornication: That every one of you should know how to possess his vessel in sanctification and honor;*" (See also verses 5–8)

   "*I beseech you therefore, brethren, by the mercies of God, that ye present your bodies a living sacrifice, holy, acceptable unto God, which is your reasonable service.*" Romans 12:1

   Since carnality has to do with the nature of the flesh, is a married woman carnal when she is intimate with her husband? 1 Corinthians 7:34–35

   No. "*There is a difference also between a wife and a virgin. The unmarried woman careth for the things of the Lord, that she may be holy both in body and in spirit: but she that is married careth for the things of the world, how she may please her husband. And this I speak for your own profit: not that I may cast a snare upon you, but for that which is comely, and that ye may attend upon the Lord without distraction.*"

   Remember in a previous lesson that all three loves, Agape, Phileo and Eros are perfect in the sight of God in a marriage. Marriage between one man and one woman is a perfect way to escape from fornication and adultery. Carnality has not been profitable overall in people's lives.

2. Why is it a profit for us to remain a virgin until we are married? see 1 Corinthians 7:36

   "*But if any man think that he behaveth himself uncomely toward his virgin, if she pass the flower of her age, and need so require, let him do what he will, he sinneth not: let them marry.*"

   The profit is that we don't sin against God, and that we avoid getting hurt and used. A man that appreciates our virginity, will marry us, we belong to him. We are 'his virgin'. A Christian man should appreciate that our virginity is a gift to him from God. And women believe it is meant for us to give to our husband upon marriage. Saving ourselves for marriage is a very good reason to date Christians who would be more prone to appreciate our chaste behavior. Think about the joy and confidence our husbands would have in us, which would be the building block of an entire life together in a bond of trust. He won't ever need to concern himself that we might be desiring an old boyfriend. 'You are his', not for oppression or possession but in appreciation, trust, and as scripture calls it, cleaving together. Further discussion is made for us in this section if any of us has not remained a virgin.

Teachers, in addressing various versions of the Bible on 1 Corinthians 7:36 a few versions of the Bible state, *"If any man think he behaved himself uncomely against his virgin 'daughter'.* The word 'daughter' is not in the original Greek text or in most versions of the Bible. Most scholars agree this bible verse is speaking to betrothed men, not fathers. They believe the key words being 'if any man' means a man should go ahead and marry if he has behaved improperly. If he does marry, he has not sinned. It does not condone any man to have physical relations or marriage with his daughter. Today we include any parent, sister, brother, cousin, aunt, uncle, or close relative in our belief there should be no physical relations or marriage with them. See also, Deuteronomy 27: 20–23. Our sons and daughters should be taught these principles and protected from any occurrence of impropriety. Allowing children safe ways to address a parent or adult counsellor about this subject is the best option if it happened or almost happened.

3. At what age should we consider marriage?

At the time of this writing the legal age of consent in most states of the United States, is either seventeen or eighteen, in some states it is sixteen. There are states where there is also a legal option to marry or have consenting sex with someone who is three to four years older or younger.

If one is able to consent when four years younger than a sixteen year old, that means a state might have laws which say it is okay for a twelve year old to consent. Christians believe twelve years old is too young, they are a 'child'. And of course, the Bible states that sex outside of marriage is wrong whether consenting or not. Society today usually recognizes eighteen years old as the minimum age for marriage.

4. Does being carnal mean that a woman can't serve the Lord if she is married, or will she just have a distraction? See Titus 2:3–5.

No. An aged woman is meant to be a teacher of good things and hopefully teach the younger women, among other things. However, if she is married, she will need to attend to her husband and family first, so she will have a distraction. An unmarried woman should care for 'all' things of the Lord.

5. Should an aged woman or young woman be married or not for teaching Titus 2?

The Bible does not distinguish whether a woman should be married to teach the Titus 2 Woman goals. Keep in mind some women never marry or have children. Through prayer and the Holy Spirits counsel the Lord will give each of us direction to serve Him in the manner He puts on our heart. The Titus 2 teachings could be an excellent ministry for any Christian woman, to teach those younger than themselves or even to assist another teacher.

6. Is a man also supposed to be pure from carnality? In Matthew 5:28 Jesus said that even when a man thinks on a woman in lust it is wrong. These verses are also profitable for women to learn:

"I suppose therefore that this is good for the present distress, I say, that it is good for a man so to be." 1 Corinthians 7:26

Paul wrote this concerning a man being a virgin. Present distress could be from a famine in that day, or opposition to Christianity which caused persecution and death so Paul counselled that they might not want to be married or have children because of persecution. See Paul's entire writing in 1 Corinthians 7:25–40

John 3:2,3 *"Beloved, now are we the sons of God, and it doth not yet appear what we shall be: but we know that, when he shall appear, we shall be like him; for we shall see him as he is. And every man that hath this hope in him purifieth himself, even as he is pure."*

Psalms 119:9 *"Wherewithal shall a young man cleanse his way? by taking heed thereto according to thy word."*

B. To be chaste is to be governed by the Spirit of God.

1. Are women supposed to be chaste even if their husbands are not obedient to God's word? See 1 Peter 3:1,2

    "Likewise, ye wives, be in subjection to your own husbands; that, if any obey not the word, they also may without the word be won by the conversation of the wives; while they behold your chaste conversation coupled with fear."

    Conversation means the life of the wife. Her words, attitudes, care, devotion, and faith will eventually win him to the Lord which hopefully is the wife's first priority.

2. What does 1 Corinthians 6:18–20 tell me to do if someone is trying to have a sexual relationship outside of marriage?

    "Flee fornication. Every sin that a man doeth is without the body; but he that committeth fornication sinneth against his own body. What? know ye not that your body is the temple of the Holy Ghost which is in you, which ye have of God, and ye are not your own?" Remember verse 20 *"For ye are bought with a price: therefore glorify God in your body, and in your spirit, which are God's."*

3. What efforts can we make today to become chaste women? These are practical suggestions from godly Christian women as they studied this lesson.

    *   Remain a virgin until married, practicing Gods law to love Him and to love our neighbor
    *   If I am unable to contain myself, marry, hopefully to a Christian man
    *   Stay away from things that can cause envying and strife and divisions in my life, or the church
    *   Confess to Jesus and ask for forgiveness and His grace if things contrary to being chaste have occurred
    *   Remain faithful to the calling from God to be chaste, He cares for us and wants us to have a good life

4. What about my friends who are not Christians?

    "Be ye not unequally yoked together with unbelievers: for what fellowship hath righteousness with unrighteousness? and what communion hath light with darkness?" 2 Corinthians 6:14

First, be friends with other believers. Paul is speaking to the people of the church here, but it is good advice also to marry another Christian. Attempting to gain a sister to Christ, is good. But be careful when "*becoming as they are, in order that you might win some.*" Do not let others coax us into sin.

C. Being chaste but being denied purity

Because of another's 'natural' or 'carnal' disposition some have been denied their chastity. God wants the best for His children, but sometimes bad things happen to us, such as rape and strong coercing. His word says that some of us will suffer the same things as those in this world. It is important for us to know God is in control even of our suffering. He allows it to establish our lives in Him by allowing Him to work in us. He allows it for conviction of sin to the one who caused the harm. Have faith. He will strengthen us, settle us, and give us peace. Still trust and obey, knowing he loves us. See 1 Peter 5:9,10 Even our very young children can benefit from some of the knowledge we find in the passages below. Our teens should learn about them not to put fear into them but knowledge. Whether we like it or not, there are wicked people in the world who want to hurt us.

"*Whom resist stedfast in the faith, knowing that the same afflictions are accomplished in your brethren that are in the world. But the God of all grace, who hath called us unto His eternal glory by Christ Jesus, after that ye have suffered a while, make you perfect, stablish, strengthen, settle you.*"

1. What does the Bible say about rape?

    Dueteronomy 22:23–29 "*If a damsel that is a virgin be betrothed unto an husband, and a man find her in the city, and lie with her; Then ye shall bring them both out unto the gate of that city, and shall stone them with stones that they die; the damsel, because she cried not, being in the city; and the man, because he hath **humbled** his neighbour's wife: so thou shalt put away evil from among you. But if a man find a betrothed damsel in the field, and the man force her, and lie with her: then the man only that lay with her shall die: But unto the damsel thou shalt do nothing; there is in the damsel no sin worthy of death: for as when a man riseth against his neighbour, and slayeth him, even so is this matter: For he found her in the field and the betrothed damsel cried, and there was none to save her. If a man find a damsel that is a virgin, which is not betrothed, and lay hold on her, and lie with her, and they be found; Then the man that lay with her shall give unto the damsel's father fifty shekels of silver and she shall be his wife; because he hath humbled her, he may not put her away all his days.*" Cry out.

2. What did David's daughter, Tamar, do in 2 Samuel 13:11–14?

    "*And when she had brought them unto him to eat, he took hold of her, and said unto her, Come lie with me, my sister. And she answered him, Nay, my brother, do not force me; for no such thing ought to be done in Israel: do not thou this folly. And I, whither shall I cause my **shame** to go? and as for thee, thou shalt be as one of the fools in Israel. Now therefore, I pray thee, speak unto the king; for he will not withhold me from thee. Howbeit he would not hearken unto her voice: but, being stronger than she, forced her, and lay with her.*" Then he hated her, and it was greater than the love he had for her. See entire story in 2 Samuel 13.

    Tamar pleaded with Amnon not to rape her. Amnon was King David's son and her half-brother. Absalom, her full brother, took matters into his own hands killing Amnon because David would not punish him. Tamar was shamed by Amnon and remained desolate in her brother Absalom's house. To our knowledge she never married because of the trauma of this experience. Again, do not go alone, even to a relative. Plead.

3. Another event is found in Genesis 34 about Dinah. Who is Jacob and Leah's daughter. Jacob is the son of Isaac, who was the son of Abraham. When Dinah went out alone to see the daughters of the land, what did the young prince of the country do to her, when he found her alone in a field?

    He saw her, took her, and lay with her and **defiled** her. The young prince's soul then clave to Dinah and he had his father arrange their marriage. When she went to live with him, her brothers took vengeance killing all the men who were weak from circumcision, which they had asked them to do. The Prince's people had willingly subjected themselves to circumcision for the Lord. Then the brothers took the little ones and the wives of the young prince's people captive and took all their wealth and cattle and sheep. Jacob told his sons they troubled him and made him to stink before the people of the land. *Don't go alone! Run, Plead, Cry out!*

4. How can we avoid it?

    Today of course, we do not stone people to death because of rape whether she is a virgin, betrothed or married. First, don't go anywhere alone, we are to flee fornication, plead with them to stop. Then run, scream, and cry out if being raped, molested, or coerced to avoid these life altering situations. 1 Thessalonians 5:22 states to *"Abstain from all appearance of evil"*. God knows what is happening and someone might hear and come and help if you scream; this also lets others know you are against this action or attempted action. God is for punishment for this crime, and we need to know this also!

5. Who is to blame?

    A person who is raped against their will or molested as a child or young person; is not to be blamed. It is an act to humble, shame, and defile them and Satan is always behind it. It is our reaction to these events that matters. Jesus said we will have tribulation in life, just like when He was put to death on the cross. His protection for our soul is spiritual and eternal. And even if we lose one battle, we know the war against Satan has already been won by Jesus and His judgment will come! Be strong in this tribulation, pray and forgive and move on with your chaste life. Many women can attest to seeing judgement in this world, even when it took a long time to come.

6. What should we do if we know a woman that has been raped, molested, or coerced?

    If it is happening now *Run, Plead, Cry out!*

    If you or any of the women you are teaching has experienced sexual misconduct from another, please do not be defeated by these actions. Have compassion, pray, and seek medical attention as soon as possible. The medical community should help in reporting the incident to the police. God and the world agree there should be punishment for this crime. Encourage them to speak up and talk to someone, a family member, a pastor, or a mature Christian woman. Pray and help them with emotional and spiritual guidance in handling such a cruel and selfish act. Help guide them through their mourning. Yes, a mourning period will occur.

We should continue to be governed by the Spirit of God to want to do what is right even if it may be hard. Read Matt 5:44. *"But I say unto you, Love your enemies, bless them that curse you, do good to them that hate you, and pray for them which despitefully use you and persecute you;"* It won't be easy to love our enemy, but it is what we are called to do. Don't let it affect your relationship with the Lord, continue your chaste walk with Him. Be strong in the Lord, do not be defeated by this. He loves us, He died for us. He wants to prosper us, not to harm us. Remembering Jesus and His suffering is the key to gaining strength for the Christian after such an ordeal. Encourage them to be honorable and bear up under the weight of the problem. Just as in any sin problem life can throw at us; let's not let Satan have even more victories. Pray with and love them. Remind them of God's love. If possible, keep checking on them. Follow up for as long as needed. But do not to keep reminding them of what happened. Don't tell others. Just try to be there for our Christian sister. As time goes by, they will need to move on with their life.

7. Why would God allow such suffering? See 2 Corinthians 4:8–10?

"We are troubled on every side, yet not distressed; we are perplexed, but not in despair; Persecuted, but not forsaken; cast down, but not destroyed; Always bearing about in the body the dying of the Lord Jesus, that the life also of Jesus might be made manifest in our body."

Because of Adam and Eve's sin, much turmoil came about in the world. Satan was there even before they sinned, tempting them, and lying to them. God then cursed the earth. Satan is still active today even though he knows there is no hope for him. We, however, have hope in Jesus! Pray to endure the effects of sin on ourselves and our world.

8. What if someone has been tricked or deceived into a carnal act?

God says in Hosea 4:6 a *"My people are destroyed for lack of knowledge:"* The Titus 2 Woman study is meant to give us the knowledge. Remember that the Serpent tricked Eve. Probably because we women and are the weaker vessel, physically, emotionally, and sometimes spiritually. We should seek God and learn His word and will for us. Together, and as our will and His will act as one, we can grow stronger for our future.

9. What if some have purposely rejected the knowledge they had of His will and lived a carnal life?

In the old testament in Hosea 4:6b God's word says *"…because thou hast rejected knowledge, I will also reject thee, that thou shalt be no priest to me: seeing thou hast forgotten the law of thy God, I will also forget thy children."*

This is from the Old Testament but is still meant for our reproof and correction and instruction in righteousness. Pray and ask for forgiveness. Thank the Lord Jesus that today, as Christians; we have hope, grace, and forgiveness in Him and so can all people. We can pray for forgiveness and repent; taking it one day at a time changing the way we live, and then do the works meet for repentance.

10. What if some of us have led our life in carnality not knowing God's will, even if we should have, and now want to follow the Lord's direction?

Please read I Corinthians 6:9–12 Let's turn our lives over to Him in repentance, pray for forgiveness and learn of Him, remembering His sacrifice on the cross for us.

Colossians 1:21,22 *"And you, that were sometime alienated and enemies in your mind by wicked works, yet now hath he reconciled In the body of his flesh through death, to present you holy and unblameable and unreproveable in his sight:"*

Isaiah 1:18 *"…though your sins be as scarlet they shall be white as snow;…"*

Acts 26:19,20 *"Whereupon, O king Agrippa, I was not disobedient unto the heavenly vision: But shewed first unto them of Damascus, and at Jerusalem, and throughout all the coasts of Judaea, and then to the Gentiles, that they should repent and turn to God, and do works meet for repentance."*

2 Peter 3:9 *"The Lord is not slack concerning his promise, as some men count slackness; but is longsuffering to us-ward, not willing that any should perish, but that all should come to repentance."*

Philippians 3:13,14 *"Brethren, I count not myself to have apprehended: but this one thing I do, forgetting those things which are behind, and reaching forth unto those things which are before, I press toward the mark for the prize of the high calling of God in Christ Jesus."*

Though our sins are as scarlet, He will wash us white as snow. He puts our sins as far as far as east is from the west, see Ps 103:12. All grace and forgiveness are shown in the Bible to be true. We need to repent and accept his forgiveness through Jesus Christ and forget those things behind us.

D. Keeping the church, the body and bride of Christ, chaste

Scofield Bible Notes state that there are three distinctions in man. The natural man, who is the unsaved man. The spiritual man, who accepts God and His word practicing His grace and love. And the carnal man, who is a babe in Christ, understanding only the 'milk' of the word. Every Christian must examine himself through God's word and listen to those we know are of a more spiritual nature, such as our pastor's. We are to be chaste for God's sake and our church, as well for ourselves.

1. What are the carnal traits Paul describes in 1 Corinthians 3:3,4?

"For ye are yet carnal: for whereas there is among you envying, and strife, and divisions, are ye not carnal, and walk as men? For while one saith, I am of Paul; and another, I am of Apollos; are ye not carnal?"

2. If I am aware of envying, strife, and divisions in my church because some follow Christ and some are following carnality what should I do?

Galatians 6:1 *"Brethren, if a man be overtaken in a fault, ye which are spiritual, restore such an one in the spirit of meekness; considering thyself, lest thou also be tempted."*

All should be attempting spiritual growth but are not at the same levels of spirituality. Some may have to leave the church after patient attempts have been made to right acts of carnality and because of obvious sin, that they won't give up. There is a process for a hopeful restoration. *"To deliver such an one unto Satan for the destruction of the flesh, that the spirit may be saved in the day of the Lord Jesus."* 1 Corinthians 5:5

3. How sad for one of our own to be delivered to Satan. Is there another way that we can help? Read Matthew 18:15–20

These verses concern going one-on-one to them; then if they do not hear, taking two or three witnesses; and if they still do not hear, take it to the church. Remember we are now talking about offenses against the church. Which means our pastor and deacons should do the counseling from the one-on-one talk's all the way to the presenting of it to the church. They should make the determination.

When it is an offense against us personally then we should go to that person one-on-one, then with two or three witnesses, then to the church. As for taking it to the church, speak first to your husband about it, and let him decide if he should take it to the pastor or deacon before presenting it to the whole church. See 2 Corinthians 2:6–8 regarding the church restoring a truly repentant believer. God is for restoration.

4. What should I do if a separation occurs in my church? Most of the time, God prefers it not to happen.

1 Corinthians 4:5 *"Therefore judge nothing before the time, until the Lord come, who both will bring to light the hidden things of darkness, and will make manifest the counsels of the hearts: and then shall every man have praise of God."*

Keep in mind when Paul and Barnabas separated because of contention between them. The contention was about Mark, who was still in needed growth and maturity with teaching from Barnabas. He grew in his faith and later wrote the gospel of Mark. As we now know, the separation occurred for the eventual growth of the church of God.

Biblical Example of a Chaste woman: Find Elizabeth, in Luke 1

Elizabeth was the mother of John the Baptist, and the wife of Zacharias. She and her husband were both righteous before God. But Elizabeth was barren and old in age. God opened her womb to conceive, and she conceived John the Baptist. Elizabeth was filled with the Holy Spirit when her young, pregnant, cousin, Mary visited. She praised God when she recognized Mary had been the chosen vessel to bring the Savior into the world. She also called Mary 'blessed among women'. Her son John, leaped in her womb for joy when the savior in Mary's womb entered the room. Elizabeth was a prepared and chaste vessel for God's use.[3]

---

[3] Note: "Lord, Prepare Me to be a Sanctuary" by Randy Scruggs and John Thompson is a song of Hope and would be a powerful addition to this teaching. For the tune and stanza's, see a Hymnal or try to find it on the Internet.

KEEPERS AT HOME

Has anyone wondered how women have been able to stay home to raise their children and keep care of their homes? Have you wondered how important it is to keep a clean house? 2 Timothy 2:15 states that all scripture is given by inspiration of God and is profitable for doctrine, for reproof (to re-prove something), for correction, and for instruction is righteousness (doing the right thing). So, we should take care to realize God wants to show us something here. Through this lesson we will learn what God hopes for us as keepers at home.

The Greek word for <u>keepers</u> in Titus 2:5 according to Strong's Concordance is *oikouros*; stayer at home, domestically inclined. Strong also notes; a good housekeeper. Also, it shows *oikouros* is from the word, *ouros*; a <u>guard</u>; be"ware". Vine's Dictionary uses the Greek word *oikourgos*; meaning worker at home. Some say it means workers at home and guides of the household. Interestingly in I Timothy 5:14, the Greek word for <u>guide</u> is *oikodespoteo*, which means to manage and direct household affairs. Webster's says a keeper is to provide with the necessities of life. To maintain, protect, preserve, and save. *"I will therefore that the younger women marry, bear children, guide the house, give none occasion to the adversary to speak reproachfully."* 1 Tim 5:14

Home, according to Webster, is a dwelling place where one resides. In the Strong's Exhaustive Concordance, the Greek word for home in Titus 2 is *oikos*; a dwelling, a family home, house, temple.

A. Guarding the home

1. In John 10:10 what does a thief come to do?

    "The thief cometh not, but for to steal, and to kill, and to destroy:" And Jesus said, *"I am come that they might have life, and that they might have it more abundantly."*

2. What does John 10:12&13 say about the hireling?

    "But he that is an hireling, and the shepherd, whose own the sheep are not, seeth the wolf coming, and leaveth the sheep, and fleeth: and the wolf catcheth them, and scattereth the sheep. The hireling fleeth, because he is an hireling, and careth not for the sheep."

This study is not about any one person. It is about GOD and His plan for His women. Remember God's forgiveness, truth, and grace is in His Son!

3. In the above passages Jesus was talking about His church and those who are in charge of His people. Jesus' wisdom could be used in the sense of being a *guard* or to be ware (or be aware) of thieves and hirelings in our homes. What was the greater concern the elect lady and John had for her children? See 2 John 4

   "I rejoiced greatly that I found of thy children walking in truth, as we have received a commandment from the Father."

4. What is the doctrine or teaching of Christ on being a *guard*? See 2 John:5,6

   "And now I beseech thee, lady, not as though I wrote a new commandment unto thee, but that which we had from the beginning, that we love one another. And this is love, that we walk after his commandments. This is the commandment, That, as ye have heard from the beginning, ye should walk in it."

   Would anyone else be able to love our family like God? If we walk in love like we learned in a previous lesson, we too can love. A mother should pray for and guard her children's hearts.

5. What should the elect lady of 2 John do for her household? Vs 9,10

   "Whosoever trangresseth, and abideth not in the doctrine of Christ, hath not God. He that abideth in the doctrine of Christ, he hath both the Father and the Son. If there come any unto you, and bring not this doctrine, receive him not into your house, neither bid him God speed:"

   The person(s) that don't abide in the doctrines of Jesus and do not have God, will try to steal our homes spiritual sanctity. We need to be ware and on guard of who and what we let into our homes and today even what is seen or heard on TV, radio, and internet.

6. So then, if we are to *guard* our homes, Jesus understood that a home needs protection. We should protect it from thieves because someone who is hired by us will not protect our home or those in it properly. It is even more important that members of our household walk in the truth of God's love and commandments and that anyone bringing other doctrines besides the commands of Jesus should not be allowed into our homes. What does Proverbs 14:1 say we should guard against for peace in our homes? Ourselves.

   "Every wise woman buildeth her house: but the foolish plucketh it down with her own hands."

7. What are some ways a foolish woman plucketh down her own house?

   - She won't seek knowledge Proverbs 9:13 *"a foolish woman is clamorous: she is simple, and knoweth nothing."*
   - She never develops understanding Proverbs 10:21 *"…fools die for want of wisdom."*
   - She laughs at mischievous behavior Proverbs10:23 *"It is a sport to a fool to do mischief:"*
   - She causes trouble in the household Proverbs11:29 *"He that troubleth his own house shall inherit the wind: and the fool shall be servant to the wise of heart."*
   - She is hard to live with *"It is better to dwell in a corner of the housetop, than with a brawling woman in a wide house."* Proverbs 21:9

- She is known for her wrath to others Proverbs 12:16 "*A fool's wrath is presently known: but a prudent man covereth shame.*"
- She won't change her ways! Won't repent Proverbs 13:19 "*…it is abomination to fools to depart from evil.*"
- She is always certain she is right Proverbs 14:3 "*In the mouth of the foolish is a rod of pride:…*"

B. Guiding the home

To *guide* the house is to manage it. *Guide* in Webster's Dictionary means to give instructions, manage, or regulate. To 'manage' is to have charge of; direct; conduct; administer. And it says to manage is to conduct or direct affairs as one wishes, esp. by skill and tact.

1. To *rule* is to set up laws and guidelines. Rulers are the thinkers, they are leader's or persons who establish rules, laws, and guidelines. In the Christian home according to I Timothy 3:4,5 who should rule the household?

   It states one quality to be a bishop, which a Christian man should aspire to be is,

   "*One that ruleth well his own house, having his children in subjection with all gravity; (For if a man know not how to rule his own house, how shall he take care of the church of God?)*"

2. Who should *manage* or *guide* the household?

   The wife, the woman of the house should be the guide or manager, the keeper of the household.

3. What can we learn from studying about guiding the home?

   Hopefully, that we will want to please our husband and abide by the rules he establishes for our home. He should then allow us the freedom to conduct the affairs, as we are able and see fit even if it includes his help, as he is able. Allowing our husband and even encouraging him to set the rules gives him a vital role in the family and home life, as leader of his household. We should build up our husbands, as a man and the leader of the house.

C. Keeping the home. Our Work versus Housework versus His work

"*All scripture is given by inspiration of God, and is profitable for doctrine, for reproof, for correction and for instruction is righteousness:*" 2 Tim 3:16 Righteousness is doing the right thing. So, the study of the Proverbs woman in the Old Testament is good. Although the Proverbs woman was not necessarily a real biblical character. King Lemuels' (Samuel's) mother was real and is giving him advice on what makes a good wife. First, and foremost, however, is to rightly divide the word of truth and remember that we are New Testament women, upholding that which has been covered in section A and B above.

1. What does Proverbs 31 say about a virtuous woman and her home?

   - She is worthy Verse 10 "*…her price is far above rubies*"
   - She stands on her convictions Verse 11 "*The heart of her husband doth safely trust in her, so that he shall have no need of spoil.*"

- She is dedicated to her husband Verse 12 *"She will do him good and not evil all the days of her life."*
- She is a hard worker Verse 13 *"She seeketh wool, and flax, and worketh willingly with her hands."*
- She provides all she can Verse 14 *"She is like the merchants ships; she bringeth her food from afar."*
- She is giving to her workers Verse 15 *"She riseth also while it is yet night, and giveth meat to her household, and a portion to her maidens."*
- She is good at business Verse 16 *"She considereth a field, and buyeth it: with the fruit of her hands she planteth a vineyard."*
- She stays physically strong Verse 17 *"She girdeth her loins with strength, and strengtheneth her arms,"*
- She is tireless Verse 18 *"She perceiveth that her merchandise is good: her candle goeth not out by night."*
- She will do the work herself Verse 19 *"She layeth her hands to the spindle and her hands hold the distaff.*
- She is benevolent Verse 20 *"She stretcheth out her hand to the poor; yea, she reacheth forth her hands to the needy."*
- She is prudent, planning ahead Verse 21 *"She is not afraid of the snow for her household: for all her household are clothed with scarlet."*
- She takes good care of herself Verse 22 *"She maketh herself coverings of tapestry; her clothing is silk and purple."*
- She stands behind her man Verse 23 *"Her husband is known in the gates, when he sitteth among the elders of the land."*
- She makes quality products to sell Verse 24 *"She maketh fine linen, and selleth it; and delivereth girdles unto the merchant."*
- She has integrity Verse 25 *"Strength and honour are her clothing; and she shall rejoice in time to come."*
- She is a good counselor Verse 26 *"She openeth her mouth with wisdom; and in her tongue is the law of kindness."*
- She is observant and stays busy Verse 27 *"She looketh well to the ways of her household, and eateth not the bread of idleness."*
- Her reward is in 'her own' works Verse 31 *"Give her of the fruit of her hands; and let her own works praise her in the gates."*

2. Our priorities for housework can be determined from bible study. Read Mark 7:1–9

*"Then came together unto him the Pharisees, and certain of the scribes, which came from Jerusalem. And when they saw some of his disciples eat bread with defiled, that is to say, with unwashen, hands, they found fault. For the Pharisees, and all the Jews, except they wash their hands oft, eat not, holding the tradition of the elders. And when they come from the market, except they wash, they eat not. And many other things there be, which they have received to hold, **as the washing of cups, and pots, brazen vessels, and of tables**. Then the Pharisees and scribes asked him, Why walk not thy disciples according to the tradition of the elders, but eat bread with unwashen hands? He answered and said unto them, Well hath Esaias prophesied of you hypocrites, as it is written, This people honoureth me with their lips, but their heart if far from me. Howbeit in vain do they worship me, teaching for doctrines the commandments of men."*

Read Mark 7:14–16 *"And when he had called all the people unto him, he said unto them, Hearken unto me every one of you, and understand: There is nothing from without a man, that entering into him can defile him: but the things which come out of him, those are they that defile the man. If any man have ears to hear, let him hear."*

3. Do these verses mean we should not be concerned about housework?

    Of course we should be concerned, because we must live in a world that is made of dirt, it is dirty. Also, because we might want to show hospitality on occasion, but especially if our husband has established it in the rules he sets for the household. He could want an extremely clean home or might be more relaxed about it, being more concerned with comfort than cleanliness. Hopefully, we can reason together if his wishes seem too impossible to meet or we are not able to meet his concerns. Consider the standards needed for those living in the household. Would our husband or children be ashamed of the housekeeping?

4. Should women consider their home 24 hours a day?

    The Proverbs woman did but again we need to consider the very order of things from the God of order. There used to be a saying, 1. God 2. Family 3. Church 4. Country. However today, we should put Jesus as our first priority and all things will fall into place as they should.

5. When should a woman consider staying at home. Should she work from home or not work or is it okay to have a career? Do as God directs us considering the following.

    *   If we feel our home or family are being threatened
    *   If our children wouldn't be safe in the hands of a caretaker
    *   If our husband wants us to stay home
    *   If extra income is not needed
    *   If the Holy Spirit leads us to stay home
    *   If the Holy Spirit is convicting us to stay home or work from home

6. Should we be more concerned with keeping a perfect house or with the work of the good house, in other words a household of prayer and bible study, and worshipping God in Spirit and in Truth?

    A spiritual house. We aged women should not put more on our young women than they can handle. A perfect house is one thing, but a perfectly spiritual house is another.

7. How can we accomplish a spiritual home? A group of women identified these areas for application, as they studied being Keepers at Home:

    *   Read the Bible, preferably aloud before our family
    *   Pray aloud for members of our household, also for other people, having family prayer time
    *   Do daily devotions, tell Bible stories, as a family
    *   Pray at mealtimes and bedtimes as a family or with each child
    *   Take the family to church and Sunday School
    *   Sing/Praise & worship Jesus

8. Does God want a woman to think first of her family and her responsibilities at home before her career?

   Yes, but first ask, "Where *does* God fit in my home and family?" Then prayerfully consider your decision.

9. What sacrifices could we make to stay home with our children? A group of women identified these areas of financial consideration:

   • Turn down the thermostat in Winter or turn it up in Summer. Go without electricity one day a week
   • Hand down clothes, go to thrift stores or garage sales
   • Use antennas instead of cable or satellite. Use phone line instead of cell phones. Limit internet usage
   • Cut food costs by buying on sale, use coupons, grow your own food, such as chickens for eggs. Grow a garden, can, hunt, barter especially with other church members
   • Work from home to save gasoline costs, car repair, and other costs

10. According to Titus 2:3–5 what other job could a Christian woman aspire to?

    Teaching Titus 2 to younger women is a good goal to aspire to. Among other Christian and benevolent ministries. Whatever we do, we should do it for the glory of the Lord! See 1 Corinthians 10:31

D. Through conversation, speak about and make a list of suggestions aged women can give to younger women on how to use their time wisely as a housekeeper, guide, or guarding their homes.

An example from one very aged woman: Children before housework. She reasoned through her study that it is okay to have a 'lived in' house. She wished she had not been so hard on her children and stepchildren as they grew up in her home, about a perfectly clean house. It is also okay to enlist others in the household to help. Even a small child can pick up their toys and clothes.

Biblical Example of a Keeper at Home: Find Martha in Luke 10:38–42 John 10,11,12

Martha was the sister of Mary of Bethany and Lazarus. She was bogged down with serving everyone. She opened her home to Jesus and the disciples and eagerly fed and served them. She became overwhelmed and came to Jesus complaining of her sister Mary, who was not serving. Jesus loved Martha and was aware of her being careful and troubled about many things, but He had to admonish her that she had not chosen wisely on where to place her priorities. Mary spent her time listening to Jesus's teachings, and He told Martha that Mary had chosen the thing that would not be taken from her, His word. Martha must have started listening to Jesus because when Lazarus died, she met Jesus on the road and said that she knew Lazarus would rise again in the resurrection. But that if Jesus had been there her brother would not have died. At that, Jesus performed the miracle of raising Lazarus from the dead, and many believed in Him.

Look up and read the verses for the following New Testament Women.

	What was her work?	Was work in the home or outside the home?	Was she married? Have children?
Anna, Luke 2:36	Served God with fasting and prayer, night, and day	In the temple	She was widowed for 84 years; had been married for 7 years Unknown children
Dorcas, Acts 9:36–43	Many good works, also made clothes for believers, etc.	Most likely in her home but might have had an outside business	Unknown
Euodias, Phillipians 4:2,3	Labored in the gospel	Outside the home	Unknown
Joanna & Susanna, Luke 8: 1–3	Ministered to Jesus of their substance	Outside of the home and in their homes, providing funds necessary for Jesus and disciples	Unknown
Lydia, Acts 16:14,15	Was a seller of Purple and opened her heart and her home	Both, providing funds necessary for Jesus and disciples and opening her home	Unknown
Mary & Martha, Luke 10:38–41, John 12:1–3	Ministered to and learned from Jesus and possibly the disciples also	Both, speaking to others of Jesus and taking Jesus and others into their home	Unknown
Priscilla, Acts 18:1–3	Expounded on the word to Apollos with her husband Aquila and ministered to Paul. She was a tentmaker.	Both, she helped Aquila and Paul with tent making. And took Paul into their home	Married to Aquila Unknown children
Rhoda, Acts 12:13	A damsel, a young girl bond servant, who served in the home of Mary, John Mark's mother and who was overjoyed at the release of Peter from prison	In the house, she was a bond servant. Learning of Jesus, she was obedient to her elders and served the praying guests	It is not known but she was probably not married or had any children

Chloe, 1 Corinthians 1:11	Her household wrote Paul for advice concerning Christian behavior.	Unknown, Paul wrote 1&2 Corinthians to address the issues they had in their church	Probably both, as addressed in Paul's letters to her household See I & 2 Corinthians
Eunice & Lois **2 Timothy 1:5, Acts 16:1**	Mother and Grandmother to Timothy probably helping him in his ministries	Unknown	Children (Timothy)

Each of these women are known from the Bible but *not* because of their husbands! And only Eunice and Lois are known for Timothy.

GOOD

The word Good in this Titus 2 passage means for us to be good. To be good we need to know what good is, who is good, and how we can be good. According to Strong's Concordance this word, good, which is translated from the Greek word *agathos*, is to be of benefit, good, well. It also has ties to the word *kalos* meaning; beautiful, better, fair, good(ly), honest, valuable, worthy. Vine's Dictionary says good is to be of benefit, good, well. Webster's Dictionary defines it as having positive or desirable qualities, superior or high quality, genuine and real, among other similar definitions. Let's study this out more and hopefully one day fulfill this trait of being good.

A. Who is Good?

1. Who did Jesus say is good in Matthew 19:17?

   "And he said unto him, Why callest thou me good? there is none good but one, that is, God: but if thou wilt enter into life, keep the commandments."

2. What does 2 Thessalonians 1:11 say about God's goodness?

   "Wherefore also we pray always for you, that our God would count you worthy of this calling, and fulfil all the good pleasure of his goodness, and the work of faith with power:"

3. What does 2 Thessalonians 2:16,17 say about His hope for us?

   "Now our Lord Jesus Christ himself, and God, even our Father, which hath loved us, and hath given us everlasting consolation and good hope through grace, Comfort your hearts, and stablish you in every good word and work."

4. See the following verses and their qualities. Studying God's goodness is an example for us to be *good*.

   - Psalms 25:8 *"Good and upright is the LORD: therefore will he teach sinners in the way."*
   - Psalms 54:6 *"I will freely sacrifice unto thee: I will praise thy name, O LORD; for it is good."*
   - Psalms 69:16 *"Hear me, O LORD; for thy lovingkindness is good: turn unto me according to the multitude of thy tender mercies."*

This study is not about any one person. It is about GOD and His plan for His women. Remember God's forgiveness, truth, and grace is in His Son!

- Psalms 86:5 *"For thou, Lord, art good, and ready to forgive; and plenteous in mercy unto all them that call upon thee."*
- Psalms 100:5 *"For the LORD is good; his mercy is everlasting; and his truth endureth to all generations."*
- Psalms 119:39 *"Turn away my reproach which I fear: for thy judgments are good."*
- Psalms 119:68 *"Thou art good, and doest good; teach me thy statutes."*
- Psalms 143:10 *"Teach me to do thy will; for thou art my God: thy spirit is good; lead me into the land of uprightness."*
- Psalms 145:9 *"The LORD is good to all: and his tender mercies are over all his works."*

B. Good is that which in its character or constitution is beneficial in its effect. What good things can we learn from the following verses?

1. In Proverbs 18:22 what good thing is spoken of there?

   "Whoso findeth a wife findeth a good thing, and obtaineth favour of the Lord."

   Paul says in 1 Cor 7:26 that in their present distress, it is good for a man to remain unmarried. However, Paul also says that it is better to marry than to burn 1 Corinthians 7:9. (Burn with passion)

2. What does Romans 12:9 tell us Christians to do which is good?

   "Let love be without dissimulation . Abhor that which is evil; cleave to that which is good." Dissimulation is hypocrisy.

3. Who does Galatians 6:10 say we should be good to?

   "As we have therefore opportunity, let us do good unto all men, especially unto them who are of the household of faith."

4. Romans 12:21 states, *"Be not overcome of evil, but overcome evil with good."* Gen 4:6,7 speaks of Cain's offering not being accepted by God and Abel's sacrifice was accepted. What can happen when we don't overcome evil with good?

   "And the LORD said unto Cain, Why art thou wroth? And why is thy countenance fallen? If thou doest well, shalt thou not be accepted? and if thou doest not well, sin lieth at the door...."

5. What does Philippians 4:8 say?

   "Finally, brethren, whatsoever things are true, whatsoever things are honest, whatsoever things are just, whatsoever things are pure, whatsoever things are lovely, whatsoever things are of good report; if there be any virtue, and if there be any praise, think on these things."

6. What about people that are good, but aren't Christian?

   Righteousness is from God and Christians are righteous only by faith in Christ who imputes His righteousness to us. He gives us the power over sin and Satan, it is not of ourselves. People who think they are righteous or those who have led good lives have their own form of godliness not

71

knowing that true righteousness is in God alone. Those emulating a righteous life need to know that not acknowledging our righteousness is only from God and not ourselves could cause others to be led away from the Lord, because as Isaiah 64:6 states *"all our righteousnesses are as filthy rags"* before God. 2 Timothy 3:5–7 says they are the people who are,

"Having a form of godliness, but denying the power thereof: from such turn away. For of this sort are they which creep into houses, and lead captive silly women laden with sins, led away with divers lusts, Ever learning, and never able to come to the knowledge of the truth".

These people leading away silly women could have ulterior motives or want influence over them. Let us not be silly women! We are clothed in the Righteousness of Christ when we accept Him as our Savior.

C. Good is a person of an honest heart…an attitude which is pleasing to God and has a good effect on others.

1. In Matthew 12:35 what good things are spoken of by Jesus?

   "A good man out of the good treasure of the heart bringeth forth good things: and an evil man out of the evil treasure bringeth forth evil things."

2. Should we try to be good and do good for others sake?

   Proverbs 11:23 *"The desire of the righteous is only good: but the expectation of the wicked is wrath."*

   Proverbs 13:21 *"Evil pursueth sinners: but to the righteous good shall be repayed."*

3. What does Proverbs 22:1 say about a good name?

   "A good name is rather to be chosen than great riches, and loving favour rather than silver and gold."

4. What does the Proverbs woman do to her husband? See Proverbs 31:12

   "She will do him good and not evil all the days of his life."

   and Proverbs 31:18

   "She perceiveth that her merchandise is good: her candle goeth not out by night."

5. What is the purpose of being good?

   "That the communication of thy faith may become effectual by the acknowledging of every good thing which is in you in Christ Jesus." Philemon 6

6. Should we want to be 'good'? Why or why not?

This is personal and is a matter of the heart, it can be kept personal, *"the spirit indeed is willing, but the flesh is weak"* Matthew 26:41. Ask if the study is helping them to be strengthened. Remind women we will be known by our fruits, love, joy, peace, longsuffering (patience),gentleness, goodness, faith, meekness, and temperance.

7. Who benefits from our being good?

    God benefits from our being good, His name will be exalted. Also, our families and the church of God will benefit.

8. What are good works?

    a. Becoming right with God

        1. loving God, loving others
        2. our own salvation, then baptism
        3. Bible Study, prayer and growth in knowledge, love, and grace

    b. Doing right before God

        1. taking care of our own husbands and children, households
        2. ministering to the needs of other Christians, helping the poor, visiting the elderly, the sick
        3. being a teacher: Sunday school, teaching other women or other church ministries
        4. helping at church

    c. Doing the right thing and spreading the Gospel of Jesus by

        1. reaching the lost, leading others to Jesus' saving grace
        2. ministering to the needs of the world, helping the poor in this world
        3. visiting the elderly and the sick, in this world

Biblical Example of being Good: Find Dorcas, in Acts 9:36–43

Dorcas was a Christian at Joppa, a church started by Phillip. She was well known for her good works of charity, sewing clothes for widows and the poor. When she died, Christians at Joppa mourned her passing greatly because she had done so much good for them. The Apostle Peter saw that other Christians loved her and that she provided for their needs. Then Peter, through the power of the Holy Spirit given to him, raised her from the dead. Many others were reported to have then believed on Jesus.

XIV

OBEDIENT TO THEIR OWN HUSBANDS

The Greek word for obedient in Strong's Concordance is *hupotasso*, it means to subordinate; reflexively, to obey, be under obedience, put under, subdue unto, be subject to, submit ourself unto. In Webster's Dictionary it means to 'be willing to obey,' while Vine's Dictionary says to yield, retire, withdraw, apparently if in disagreement. God is asking His women to consider His plan for the family unit and to allow their husbands to be the ruler over them. If we want to fulfill His plan, it is a good idea to marry someone that we can reason with and are willing to allow to rule over us. That is also why we should marry our friend; our friend will not take advantage of this call of obedience to them. Remember, this is God's plan.

The systems put into place in the world do not care about God's plan. But even these world systems have implemented give and take relations. Someone needs to take this position of leadership or ruling. Just as someone needs to be the leader in every relationship whether it is at the workplace or church, in government or in organizations. Consider the peace it would bring in our homes, our marriage, and family to allow our husband to be the ruler. Keep in mind, God did not tell men to make sure their wives obey. He asks women to obey willingly, it is not an unreasonable request.

"Wives, submit yourselves unto your own husbands, as it is fit in the Lord." The main purpose of this verse is that we should not submit to other men, but to our "own" husband, and then only as God's word allows. The Bible uses the phrase "your own husband" in references to submitting or obeying in Ephesians 5:22, Titus 2:5, Colossians 3:18, and 1 Peter 3:1 and 5. These verses show it is evident God is serious about this.

The Bible does not specifically state that we have to be obedient to anyone except God, His word, and our husbands, also our parents when we are young. We are taught in Scripture to give honor to our parents, pastors, and elders in the church and those that have rule over us, such as government and its law. Unless they disagree with the Word of God. We should, however, submit to God and our own husbands first. Then, as Christians, Ephesians 5:21 *"submitting yourselves one to another in the fear of God"* to keep peace in the family of God.

This study is not about any one person. It is about GOD and His plan for His women. Remember God's forgiveness, truth, and grace is in His Son!

A. To be obedient to our husband is to listen to him and attend to him, go along with him and his decisions. Being obedient does not mean we have no voice. It is okay to reason together. Just as God said in Isaiah 1:18 *"Come now, and let us reason together…"*. If God wants to reason with us, Christians also should reason with their spouses and each other. But once our husband makes a final decision; his decisions need to be backed by us.

1. 1 Peter 3:5 tells us, that holy women in old times obeyed their husbands, what gave them the strength?

    "For after this manner in the old time the holy women also, who trusted in God, adorned themselves, being in subjection unto their own husbands:" Their trust in God gave them strength.

2. All Christians, including our husbands, should look on the things of others. Yes, even their wives. Protecting our families' hearts, minds, bodies, and souls. What attitudes in Philippians 2:3,4 should we put in practice in our life and hope for our husband?

    "Let nothing be done through strife or vainglory; but in lowliness of mind let each esteem other better than themselves. Look not every man on his own things, but every man also on the things of others."

3. How do the following verses help us learn how to respond to our husbands?

    Proverbs 15:1 *"A soft answer turneth away wrath: but grievous words stir up anger."*

    Ephesians 5:33 *"Nevertheless let every one of you in particular so love his wife even as himself; and the wife see that she reverence her husband."*

    Reverence, in Greek, is the word "phobeo" and means to be in awe, revere, be sore afraid. Webster says it is a feeling or attitude of deep respect, love, and awe, as for something sacred. Our vows are sacred before God.

B. Obedience is to fulfill what we have heard from our own husbands, to submit to him before anyone else, except God.

1. Does Colossians 3:18 back up the above statement? What does it say?

    Yes. *"Wives, submit yourselves unto your own husbands, as it is fit in the Lord."*

2. In 1 Corinthians 14:35 how can a Christian woman show her obedience to her own husband, when at church?

    "And if they will learn anything, let them ask their husbands at home: for it is a shame for women to speak in the church."

    And Verse 40 *"Let all things be done decently and in order."*

    Most women agree, that during Sunday School, if the teacher and their husbands are okay with it, they can speak up. Asking our husband at home also keeps from embarrassing him if he does not have an answer and then he can consider and study out the answer first.

One Christian woman in our study group once told of when she asked her Sunday School teacher a question about the Bible and was told to go ask her husband. She was puzzled by this since her teacher knew her husband didn't attend church. She was certain her husband wouldn't know the answer if she didn't. She had attended Bible College, her husband hadn't. But she did go home and ask her husband the theological question and much to her surprise he got out a Bible and studied to find the answer for her. Her Sunday School Teachers request became effective. Her husband then began studying the Bible and attending church regularly. He is now a Sunday School Teacher and Deacon in the church. God alone had arranged this sequence of events and knew what was best for our friend and her husband.

3. What if a woman is not married, does she need to obey anyone? From whom should she obtain guidance?

    A woman's father should be obeyed, if, if she lives in his household. A Christian father could still be consulted even if a woman is not living in his house and her husband approves of his consultation. There is no recommendation for not consulting others, Proverbs 24:6 says

    "…and in the multitude of counsellors there is safety".

    If a woman does not have a Christian husband or father; it is acceptable for her to ask her pastor or deacon or Sunday School teacher to answer any questions they have regarding their studies in the Lord, ministries, or direction for their life. An older godly woman in the church is also an acceptable choice for counsel. However, they should not interrupt in the middle of a church service, or as good manners has it, during preaching or a speech.

    A good ideal is to always have another person present when asking questions especially if asking members of the opposite sex a question. This will avoid the appearance of evil or of doing evil. It protects ourselves and our pastor, teacher, or anyone else involved in a possible misunderstanding. Aged women should also request the presence of another person when counselling, to avoid confusion. Never forget to pray and ask God for His guidance first. Another great lesson to learn and remember is that a person should not take criticism from anyone they would not take advice from. Christians should have our best interest at heart and give us the best advice.

4. According to Ephesians 5:22 to whom should Christian women submit?

    "Wives, submit yourselves unto your own husbands, as unto the Lord."

5. According to 1 Timothy 3:2 and 1 Timothy 3:12 who should be the husband of one wife?

    Bishops and Deacons, which is a good goal for all men of God. Your pastor should be consulted if a divorced person is acting as Bishop or Deacon.

6. And who should they rule well? See 1 Timothy 3: 4 and 1Timothy 3:12

    They should rule their households and their children well. Vine's Dictionary states that to rule is to stand before or to lead. Strong's concordance shows the Greek word *proistemi* for the word rule which means to stand before (in rank), preside, maintain, be over. Therefore, it is for the husband to set the rules or standards he expects of his household and children. Here is an area a wife needs to submit to her husband. We should discuss these things with our future husband before we marry. It is best to know in advance our roles and expectations of each other. If discussing the rules before marriage didn't happen, do it now to avoid future misunderstandings.

7. What does Genesis 2:24 say a man should do when he is married?

"Therefore shall a man leave his father and his mother and shall cleave unto his wife: and they shall be one flesh." Leave and cleave! A man is subject only to God once he leaves his parent's home. Of course, governments do still have laws and regulations they should follow.

8. What is the limit to my husband's commands? See Ephesians 5:25

"Husbands, love your wives, as Christ also loved the church, and gave himself for it;"

So Christian men should be willing to love us enough to die for us. So, any demands our husband makes of us should also be from love, a dying love for us. If his demands come from love his demands should be a small thing to listen to and submit to by doing as he asks. God loves a cheerful giver and our husbands would appreciate that too. We should try to do our best. The limit is when or if it fails to meet with God's word or His commandments or the laws of our society, which are there for our protection as well as for His glory.

9. Should we be offended that God wants us to be obedient and submissive?

It seems as we have previously discussed in the lesson on "Love" that to submit (and obey) from a New Testament biblical perspective is to submit to another's love. God's love and our husbands love. Again, just like we studied in a previous lesson; the love and submission seem to be so intertwined that if we have doubts about obeying, our love might not yet be perfected toward God. Keep in mind, Christ humbled himself and submitted himself to the cross, He became obedient unto death even the death of the cross. *"God so loved the world, that He gave His only begotten Son, that whosoever believeth in Him should not perish, but have everlasting life."* John 3:16 Hopefully, your husband will not take advantage of the call for your obedience to him and expect nothing from you but in the spirit of love, which makes it easier for you to obey and submit.

10. What if a woman cannot be obedient to an unfaithful husband or her husband is too demanding, or for some other reason they want to divorce?

God knows the reasons for talking about divorce. It is not His will for married couples to be separated from one another but for fasting and prayer. 1 Corinthians 7:5 *"Defraud ye not one the other, except it be with consent for a time, that ye may give yourselves to fasting and prayer; and come together again, that Satan tempt you not for your incontinency."*

- If she has been physically abused, go to a doctor or emergency room.
- Pray with her, it could be an opportunity for them to grow closer to the Lord.
- Help them remember what made the couple fall in love in the first place.
- Remind them that for the sake of their children she and her spouse should try to restrain from showing too much emotion in front of them.

- Remind her that she is still the responsible adult/parent and not let or have the children assume that role.
- She should hopefully, seek reconciliation and restoration until a divorce has been finalized and one of them has remarried. Our God is a God of reconciliation and restoration just as He reconciled with us.
- In the case of adultery, a couple might have biblical authority to divorce, but they should consult a pastor about it. Christian counselling could be recommended. Forgiveness is always possible; the Lord wants us to forgive. Just like He forgave us. Jesus is in the business of forgiveness. True repentance is the key to true reconciliation.

11. How should we give guidance if confronted by a person seeking advice concerning their marriage or divorce?

It is best for couples to seek counselling from a pastor, who would have a better understanding of God's will in this matter. Old Testament guidelines are found in Deuteronomy 22: 20–22 and Deuteronomy 26: 1–4

If drawn into counselling. Let her do all the talking; knowing there are always two sides to a relationship and both parties have their side of their marriage issues. Although others can sympathize with the hurt of such an action, we Christians can pray with and for them. Always remember that we are not to be busy bodies in other people's matters, confidentiality is expected, especially, in our own relationship or future relationships to both parties.

To prevent it from happening in the first place, it is important to remember we cannot change our spouses, but God can. However, we can examine ourselves now, as we should throughout our marriage, and remember the lessons we have been taught from our study. Here are a few examples shared from godly women when studying this lesson:

- Scripture says unbelieving husbands will eventually be won to the Lord by our conversation (life)
- Pray for them
- Do not carry idols into our marriage
- Do not commit adultery
- Encourage and build up our spouse
- Stop criticizing our spouse or their ways, stop complaining
- Do not usurp authority over our husbands
- Let our husbands be the family leader. See 1 Corinthians 7:10 The husband is accountable, even as an unbeliever, for the spiritual leadership of his family before God. We will all stand before God one day.

Biblical Example of being Obedient to our own Husbands:
Find Sarah in Genesis 11–25, 49:31 Hebrews 11

Sarah was the wife of Abraham. God promised Abraham a child. After years of trying to have a child and being a very aged woman, Sarah encouraged Abraham to have a child through Hagar, her Egyptian servant. When Sarah gave her servant Hagar to Abraham, she must have feared that because of her age the promised child was not going to come from her. The law had not yet been given so Sarah might not have known she should not put her trust in her own way, or the way of the people in that day. However, Abraham agreed to this arrangement, which has caused turmoil in the world, affecting lives even today. Hagar had a son, Ishmael. Ishmael's descendants are thought to have begun the Islamic/Muslim religion. God later told Abraham and Sarah that she would have the promised child and Sarah finally placed her faith in God and when she was ninety years old, she bore the child, Isaac. Still, she always obeyed her husband, giving Abraham reverence even calling him, 'lord'. 1 Peter 3:6 says we are the daughters of Sarah as long as we do well and are not afraid with any amazement. Sarah is listed as one of the faithful in what is called the 'Hall of Faith' in Hebrews 11.

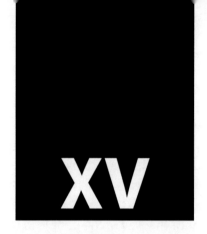

XV

THAT THE WORD OF GOD BE NOT BLASPHEMED

According to Strong's concordance, the Greek word for blasphemed, is *blasphemeo* and it means to vilify, speak impiously about, to defame, rail on, revile, and to speak evil of. Webster says it means, to speak in a way that shows irreverence for God or something sacred. Today, we hear blaspheme about God on television, the radio, and in everyday conversations. Even from the people we are closest to. We need to stand up for God and His standards, building strength, and backing each other. There is a saying that "we are only as strong as our weakest link". It is not a biblical saying, but it conveys the principle that as the weaker vessels we should show God's glory in us by doing as He says and teaching and strengthening each other. Let us do all we can to bring Him glory by respecting ourselves and each other and reverencing Him.

A. God holds the highest standards for His Word. His Word is above even His name. He sets the standard for our lives through His Word. Too many of His children have been sifted like wheat because of lack of knowledge of His Word.

1. According to John 1:1 what is the Word of God?

   "In the beginning was the Word, and the Word was with God, and the Word was God."

2. What does John 1:14 say about God's word?

   "And the Word was made flesh, and dwelt among us, (and we beheld his glory, the glory as of the only begotten of the Father,) full of grace and truth."

3. And what does Psalms 138:2 say about His word?

   "I will worship toward thy holy temple, and praise thy name for thy lovingkindness and for thy truth: for thou hast magnified thy word above all thy name."

4. And Philippians 2:9 states that His name, Jesus, is above all names.

   "Wherefore God also hath highly exalted him, and given him a name which is above every name."

This study is not about any one person. It is about GOD and His plan for His women. Remember God's forgiveness, truth, and grace is in His Son!

5. Revelations 19:13

   "…and his name is called The Word of God."

6. From 2 Timothy 2:15 what does God want us to do with His Word?

   "Study to shew thyself approved unto God, a workman that needeth not to be ashamed, rightly dividing the word of truth." The first division of the Bible is between Old Testament and New Testament.

B. His Word has the power to change lives. He is our hope, our anchor, our creator, our savior. God wants to help His church *"That he might sanctify and cleanse it with the washing of water by the word".* Ephesians 5:26

1. Has the study of the Titus 2 Woman shown that God's ways are not like the ways of the world?

   Yes. Give examples.

   God wants us to learn of Him and follow Him. He wants us to have help from other Christians. The world leaves us without much direction and with little understanding and gives no hope but for things that perish. Even our mothers might not know scripture or are afraid to teach us or speak of things that could help us understand. They often scold us but do not give actual scripture that can encourage us and build us up to help us know these directions are truly from God. But still, grace and forgiveness are what we need to exhibit toward the people we feel should have taught us these lessons. Let's help each other stand firm in faith and hope in God to accomplish His will in us.

2. Has the study of the Titus 2 Woman shown God has the best intentions for us to live a good life?

   Yes, He does. Hopefully, you realize how much God loves you and that He wants you to be happy, live full lives and be filled with His love and grace.

   "But whoso keepeth his word, in him verily is the love of God perfected: hereby know we that we are in him". 1 John 2:5

3. Has the Titus 2 Woman study been helpful?

   Hopefully we all have gained knowledge, and a deeper understanding of God's will for us and developed a deeper relationship with God. And lifetime friendships with the other Christian women who have taught or studied with us and shared their experiences and love.

4. Did the study show that a Christian woman can bring glory to God? Her family? The church?

   Absolutely. God should be foremost in the thoughts and actions of all His people, and our efforts will be rewarded by Him.

5. List the areas needing to be changed in your life and what you need to bring into subjection to His word since studying the Titus 2 Woman.

   Areas that need to be changed is personal for each person, they don't need to share this with anyone, but God. But the Word does say, to confess your sins one to another and this is a good time to do that. If asked for help to change an area of a woman's life, please pray and do what you can to help, in love.

6. Remember from the introduction of this study guide what to do if brought under conviction? What was that?

   Repent and ask forgiveness, do works meet for repentance. And remember the Titus 2 Woman study isn't about any one person it is about God and His plan for His women. Even though it can get personal. Remember forgiveness, truth, and grace in His Son!

C. Not following God's Word would bring blasphemy against it. It would cause others to speak evil of it.

1. In our world today our society has blasphemed God and His word. How can we Christian women avoid bringing blaspheme against God's Word?

   Follow what has been outlined in the Titus 2 Woman study or anything the Bible requests of us, out of love for Jesus.

2. Could women who profess to be Christians but do not follow God's plan be responsible for the world's blasphemy against God and His word?

   Yes. And that is very painful to know. All Christians have an enemy that does not want us to succeed in our walk with God. If we are guilty only repentance, asking for forgiveness and pressing on toward the mark of the high calling of God, in Christ Jesus, can change the world's opinion of God, His Word and us.

3. How should we react to those who would speak evil of us and God's Word?

   Tell them the truth, in love, and if they will not hear recognize they are not interested in eternal life. Read Acts 13:45–46 *"But when the Jews saw the multitudes, they were filled with envy, and spake against those things which were spoken by Paul, contradicting and blaspheming. Then Paul and Barnabas waxed bold, and said, It was necessary that the word of God should first have been spoken to you: but seeing ye put it from you, and judge yourselves unworthy of everlasting life, lo, we turn to the Gentiles."* The Gentiles were glad about this and glorified the word of the Lord and many believed. Read verses 50–52 to see what happened next.

4. How should I react to Christian's who bring about blasphemy against God's Word? Galatians 6:1

   "Brethren, if a man be overtaken in a fault, ye which are spiritual, restore such an one in the spirit of meekness; considering thyself, lest thou also be tempted."

D. Following God's Word; a list of attributes.

1. Hebrews 4:12 *"For the word of God is quick, and powerful, and sharper than any twoedged sword, piercing even to the dividing asunder of soul and spirit, and of the joints and marrow, and is a discerner of the thoughts and intents of the heart."*

2. James 1:22–25 *"But be ye doers of the word, and not hearers only, deceiving your own selves. For if any be a hearer of the word, and not a doer, he is like unto a man beholding his natural face in a glass: for he beholdeth himself, and goeth his way, and straightway forgetteth what manner of man he was. But whoso looketh into the perfect law of liberty, and continueth therein, he being not a forgetful hearer, but a doer of the work, this man shall be blessed in his deed."*

3. 1 John 2:5,6 *"But whoso keepeth his word, in him verily is the love of God perfected: hereby know we that we are in him. He that saith he abideth in him ought himself also so to walk, even as he walked."*

4. Revelations 3:10 *"Because thou hast kept the word of my patience, I also will keep thee from the hour of temptation, which shall come upon all the world, to try them that dwell on the earth."*

5. Revelations 6:9 *"And when he had opened the fifth seal, I saw under the altar the souls of them that were slain for the word of God, and for the testimony which they held:"*

6. Revelations 19:13 *"And he was clothed with a vesture dipped in blood: and his name is called The Word of God."*

Biblical Example of Women who do not bring blaspheme against God's Word: Willing vessels. Hopefully, you and me, and all Christian Women around the world. Now is the time to be all we can be in Him and for Him!

A Closing Prayer of Gratitude

"Thank you, our Dear Heavenly Father, our Creator and our Lord and Savior, Jesus. You who are the author and finisher of our faith. We thank You for the wisdom found only in You and Your word. Thank You for Your love and willingness to come and set us free from the penalty of our sin by Your death, burial, and resurrection. And thank You Holy Spirit of God for leading us in the truths of this ministry and the joy You give us by exalting Jesus in us. Though our souls were convicted about our failings and our spirits mourned, through Your grace, You were making these truths become a peaceable fruit to us. Lord Jesus, please use this study as a tool to further Your will in the lives of Your women and Your work in and among us. We ask that You exhort, encourage, and build up all Your women in knowledge, love, and in the grace, You have given us. Give us confidence in our walk with you, Lord. Amen"

QUALITIES OF CHARITY 1 CORINTHIANS 13:4–8 ACTS OF SUBMITTING TO ANOTHERS LOVE	SPOUSE TALKING POINTS	CHILDREN TALKING POINTS
1. **Suffereth Long** (is patient) *"Strengthened with all might, according to his glorious power, unto all patience and longsuffering with joyfulness;" Colossians 1:11* *"Knowing this, that the trying of your faith worketh patience." James 1:3*		
2. **Is Kind** *"And they spake unto him, saying, If thou be kind to this people, and please them, and speak good words to them, they will be thy servants for ever." 2 Chron. 10:7 (see also Psalms 63:3)* *"And be ye kind one to another, tenderhearted, forgiving one another, even as God for Christ's sake hath forgiven you." Ephesians 4:32*		
3. **Envieth Not** (not jealous or resentful of another's possessions or qualities) *"Let us walk honestly, as in the day; not in rioting or drunkenness, not in chambering or wantonness, not in strife and envying." Romans 13:13* *"Let us not be desirous of vain glory, provoking one another, envying one another." Galations 5:26*		
4. **Vaunteth not itself** (not boastful) *"Even so the tongue is a little member, and boasteth great things. Behold, how great a matter a little fire kindleth." James 3:5* *"Finally, brethren, whatsoever things are true, whatsoever things are lovely, whatsoever things are honest, whatsoever things are just, whatsoever things are pure, whatsoever things are lovely, Whatsoever things are of good report; if there by any virtue, and if there be any praise, think on these things." Philippians 4:8*		

QUALITIES OF CHARITY 1 CORINTHIANS 13:4–8 ACTS OF SUBMITTING TO ANOTHERS LOVE	SPOUSE TALKING POINTS	CHILDREN TALKING POINTS
5. **Is not puffed up** (not proud, Submission=humility) *"Take my yoke upon you, and learn of me; for I am meek and lowly in heart: and ye shall find rest unto your souls." Matthew 11:29* *"Let nothing be done through strife or vainglory; but in lowliness of mind let each esteem other better than themselves" Philippians 2:3*		
6. **Does not behave itself unseemly** (is not rude, avoids the appearance of evil. Submission is to…learn so you never fall) *"Abstain from all appearance of evil. And the very God of peace sanctify you wholly; and I pray God your whole spirit and soul and body be preserved blameless unto the coming of our Lord Jesus Christ." 1 Thessalonians 5:22,23* *"And beside this giving all diligence, add to your faith virtue; and to virtue knowledge; and to knowledge temperance; and to temperance patience; and to patience godliness; and the godliness brotherly kindness; and to brotherly kindness charity. For if these things be in you, and abound, they make you that shall neither be barren nor unfruitful in the knowledge of our Lord Jesus Christ." 2 Peter 1:5–8*		
7. **Seeketh not her own** (is not self-seeking, not selfish. Submission is to acknowledge His sacrifice) *"I will freely sacrifice unto thee: I will praise thy name, O LORD; for it is good" Psalms 54:6* *"That if thou shalt confess with thy mouth the Lord Jesus, and shalt believe in thine heart that God hath raised him from the dead, thou shalt be saved." Romans 10:9*		

QUALITIES OF CHARITY 1 CORINTHIANS 13:4–8 ACTS OF SUBMITTING TO ANOTHERS LOVE	SPOUSE TALKING POINTS	CHILDREN TALKING POINTS
8. Is not easily provoked (not angered or not angered easily like to the point of temper tantrums, even at two or three years old). *"He that is soon angry dealeth foolishly: and a man of wicked devices is hated"* Proverbs 14:17 (see also Matt 5:22) *"A soft answer turneth away wrath: but grievous words stir up anger."* Proverbs 15:1		
9. **Thinketh no evil** (keeps no record of wrongs) *"There is therefore now no condemnation to them which are in Christ Jesus, who walk not after the flesh, but after the Spirit."* Romans 8:1 *"Brethren, I count not myself to have apprehended: but this one thing I do, forgetting those things which are behind, and reaching forth unto those things which are before, I press toward the mark for the prize of the high calling of God in Christ Jesus."* Philippians 3:13,14		
10. **Rejoices not in iniquity** (iniquity is sin) *"By this we know that we love the children of God, when we love God, and keep his commandments. For this is the love of God, that we keep his commandments: and his commandments are not grievous."* 1 John 5: 2,3 *"For godly sorrow worketh repentance to salvation not to be repented of: but the sorrow of the world worketh death."* 2 Corinthians 7:10 (see also vs 9)		

QUALITIES OF CHARITY 1 CORINTHIANS 13:4–8 ACTS OF SUBMITTING TO ANOTHERS LOVE	SPOUSE TALKING POINTS	CHILDREN TALKING POINTS
11. **Rejoices in truth** *"And ye shall know the truth, and the truth shall make you free." John 8:32* *"But speaking the truth in love, may grow up into him in all things, which is the head, even Christ." Eph 4:15 (See also Ephesians 4: 14–16)*		
12. **Beareth all things** (Beareth is to "put up with" others and the bad things that come to us. Submission is to confess our faults) *"Bear ye one another's burdens, and so fulfil the law of Christ." Galatians 6:2* *"Confess your faults one to another, and pray one for another, that ye may be healed. The effectual fervent prayer of a righteous man availeth much." James 5:16*		
13. **Believeth all things** (submission is to be confident in God and His Word) *"Wherefore also it is contained in scripture, Behold, I lay in Sion a chief corner stone, elect, precious: and he that believeth on him should not be confounded." 1 Pet 2:6 (see also John 3:16)* *"And this is the confidence that we have in him, that, if we ask any thing according to his will, he heareth us." I John 5:14*		
14. **Hopeth all things** (submission is to seek honor before God in self and others) *"Which hope we have as an anchor of the soul, both sure and stedfast, and which entereth into that within the veil;" Hebrews 6:19* *"To them who by patient continuance in well doing seek for glory and honor and immortality, eternal life." Romans 2:7*		

QUALITIES OF CHARITY 1 CORINTHIANS 13:4–8 ACTS OF SUBMITTING TO ANOTHERS LOVE	SPOUSE TALKING POINTS	CHILDREN TALKING POINTS
15. **Endureth all things** (submission is to endure chastening) *"Praise ye the Lord. O give thanks unto the Lord; for he is good: for his mercy endureth for ever." Psalms 106:1* *"If ye endure chastening, God dealeth with you as with sons; for what son is he whom the father chasteneth not?" Hebrews 12:7*		
16. **Never fails** (submission is to trust in Him) *"Heaven and earth shall pass away, but my words shall not pass away." Matthew 24:35* *"Though he slay me, yet will I trust in him:…." Job 13:15*		

SITUATIONS	KNOWLEDGE	DISCRETION Understanding, Judgement & Wisdom	PRUDENCE Planning	SOBERNESS Self-control/ Action

Printed in the United States
by Baker & Taylor Publisher Services